MW00479660

Gemini

The Ultimate Guide to an Amazing Zodiac Sign in Astrology

Your Free Gift (only available for a limited time)

Thanks for getting this book! If you want to learn more about various spirituality topics, then join Mari Silva's community and get a free guided meditation MP3 for awakening your third eye. This guided meditation mp3 is designed to open and strengthen ones third eye so you can experience a higher state of consciousness. Simply visit the link below the image to get started.

https://spiritualityspot.com/meditation

Contents

Introduction

Magazines, newspapers, and other glossy commercial items have ruined the fascinating allure of astrology. Many individuals acknowledge this as an amazing phenomenon that has also been recognized as a formal field of study. If you are one of those individuals, then you have come to the right place. This expert guide has been created so that interested readers (like yourself) can find out more about people, stars, charts, and the planets that govern us.

The most interesting aspect of astrology revolves around the prediction of one's personality via charts and signs, but we must tell you that it is not quite as simple as that. This field has been recognized as one of formal study because of the very logical nature of the predictions it makes rather than the mockery presented by various forms of media. There is a science behind it that starts from the birth/natal charts. Through the birth charts, people can pinpoint the location of the Sun, the moon, and other varied planets/stars to predict what sort of personality they will have. Birth charts were very expensive to make; as technology evolved, it became a pretty straightforward and easy task to perform. Now, you can get them from various sites online by just inputting your birth time. It is worth mentioning that this process is free!

These outlines can then help determine what traits a person is likely to inherit. These predictions are not always black and white. This is why it is so annoying to experts in the field when they see how horoscopes are presented in magazines. There is a range of signs given off of the birth chart that is employed to forecast different aspects of a person's personality. The sun signs are the twelve symbols that are most commonly depicted in western astrology. Many people already know these through their birth date, but moon signs are also utilized to predict personality, behavior, and emotion rather than basic attributes and talents related to an individual.

The focus of this book will be on a more specific topic rather than tackling the entire spectrum of this enormous field known as "astrology". The focus will be on one of the sun signs called "Gemini".

This introductory chapter will examine the significant features of this sign and why this study is fascinating. It will also discuss how to use this resource effectively by explaining the value of each of the different chapters to the subject matter.

The Gemini

May 21 to June 20 is the period that encompasses people born with the Gemini star sign. Gemini, the name itself, is not English, but Latin. The Latin translation of this word means "twins." There is a lot of truth to this translation because one of the most common personality traits that Geminis are branded with is their duality. This means that Geminis are more suggestive than other signs out there, and that what they express can be completely opposite of their mood a couple of minutes earlier. This does not mean they have difficulty deciding on what to do or have "bipolar" tendencies! It just means that their personalities are unique, as they will be more expressive of this dual nature. If you are a Gemini, then you can attest to this trait!

This section delves into common aspects related to this sign (like the duality aspect); more detailed explanations can be found in the chapters below. We will also discuss key information that all Geminis should recognize about their star sign. Without discussing such material, this guide would be incomplete.

The very first thing that Geminis should know is the symbol and the glyph commonly used to represent the star sign. There are differences between the two terms (symbol and glyph) that are explained in this session. A zodiac sign's symbol is a more graphical representation of the sign and is often represented by Greek mythology characters. In our case, the "Dioscuri" twins are often the representing symbol of the Gemini star sign. Castor and Pollux were sons of Leda but had different fathers, even though they were twins! This may sound weird and fantastical, but they prove to be a very accurate symbol since they represent two contrasting personalities. This symbol emphasizes the dual nature of this star sign.

A glyph is an elemental symbol used in many aspects of typography. People often agree upon a glyph to represent a set of symbols or characters in a complex chart or in other functions. So, zodiac charts also have their own set of glyphs, where each one represents a star sign. Many zodiac magazines and articles available in the world use the terms "symbol" and "glyph" interchangeably. We have clarified this to make it easier for the reader to understand the jargon that revolves around star signs. The glyph for the Gemini star sign is the Roman numeral two. It also characterizes this sign's dual aspect but is much easier to write/make than the symbol for this star sign. Other glyphs in the zodiac charts also hold significant meaning and can be easily decoded if pondered. For example, the Sagittarius symbol revolves around a "centaur" (also a mythical creature from Greek mythology) that is known for being an archer. Its glyph is a simple bow and arrow drawing. Now that you know about this important difference, it is time to learn more about Geminis.

Each sign is assigned a "ruling planet" through which their personality's main pattern can be derived. Ruling planets prove that zodiac signs have a major link to astrology, and learning about this connection will clear up all of your misconceptions.

Planets are the major deciding factors of everything that is expressed through the zodiac signs. This first appeared to happen when early astrologers observed the planets and their energies and drew parallels to zodiac signs and their qualities. Since Neptune, Uranus, and Pluto were not identified at that time, they were not appointed any signs. Modern astrologers have associated these newly-discovered planets with signs as this sector of science continues to grow and make new discoveries. These got matched up with the zodiac signs after the 18th century, while other older pairings have been left unchanged. These associations may keep changing as further explorations are made in this field, but an important question arises: how are planets used for interpreting zodiac signs?

To answer that question, we must examine the details that astrologers provide when looking at charts. First of all, each sign has a ruler planet (or two) whose energies and qualities are a primary influence over dimensions of someone's personality. If your sun sign is in Gemini, then your ruling planet is Mercury. Greeks first matched up planets to seasons and not to these signs. Over time, astrologers developed complex techniques that led to more specific forecasts (rather than season-long predictions). The planets are like an archive or a data set used by astrologers every time they want to interpret a natal chart. They look at constellations of planets according to their position within the sign to predict major personality traits. The ruling planet and the sign are both focal points for the astrologer when looking at house cusps in a chart. This leads us to another key element used in zodiac interpretation: "houses."

The main translation of zodiac charts depends upon "houses" that the astrologer chooses beforehand. Houses form a chart, and their positions are based on location and time rather than on a date. For example, in a birth chart, if an astrologer knows the exact time of birth, then he/she will derive a very accurate interpretation. Often, the exact time might not be known, which restricts the astrologers to using the sunrise as an instrument in house calculation. This may not yield correct results for the astrologer.

As seen in the example above, the estimation of houses in a chart depends on Earth's movement along its axis and the Sun's orbit. But the difference of opinions (mathematical differences) amongst astrologers has created numerous ways of calculating houses and thereby produced a range of different "house systems." Different traditions (cultures) had their own ways of doing things, and so had different house systems as well. For example, in the Hindu tradition, houses were known as "Bhavas." But one of the most common systems known to the western hemisphere is called the "Placidus" system.

Generally, the houses are a division of the "ecliptic" plane. This plane contains the orbit of the Sun as viewed from the Earth; many house systems also regard the movement of other stars and planets in our galaxy. The Placidus system divides the planetary and star movement above and below the horizon. This division takes place in equal-sized parts, and the number of houses is twelve. The first six houses usually denominate spaces below the horizon, and the other six are associated with being above.

Houses depend on the exact time, and so this is a time-oriented system (Astro Dentist, 2020). Giovanni Magini developed this process around the 16th century, but mathematician Placidus Titis refined it; thus, the process is named after him. The system cannot be used for regions beyond the polar circles because of mathematical complications at the time of its development.

There are many other house systems like the Koch system, Capmanus, and Regiomontanus system, but the explanation of each can take up this entire guide, taking the spotlight away from our topic. This limited explanation of houses was deemed necessary to include since it gives a historical and scientific background as to how horoscopes work.

Another insight into the history of the development of this field is reflected in an image of a traditional zodiac sign and house dial. It shows an old dial that was constructed to represent divisions according to houses depending on the time of day. The idea behind it seems to be that of a sundial. The shadow that the Sun makes seems to predict the position of time in the "plane" being used, but its correct way of functioning does not matter to us since the focus is its historical significance. It shows how far astrology has come from physical dials that needed experts to predict the positioning of planets at the time of birth to having websites that do that for you. This explanation should give the readers an immense understanding of how everything is working in the background when someone is having their horoscope predicted. So, astrologers effectively fuse the house system (relating to the Earth's axis) along with the zodiac wheel (related to the Sun's movement) to read charts and make predictions or horoscopes.

Coming back to the main topic, a connection can be made between the houses and how they relate to the signs. Each house is viewed as an area/part of life and is ruled/associated with a Sun sign (like Gemini). Many astrologers understand houses as being ruled by a sign, just like how the signs have a ruling planet. This understanding has been derived from the fact that each excels at that particular part of life (the part of life that is represented by the house).

The third house is usually considered to be ruled by the Sun sign Gemini. It has a modern title as well as a traditional Latin name. The modern title is "the House of Sharing." From the title, you may have guessed that it is related to communication. It has been rightly linked with Gemini since it has already been established that Geminis do not fear being overly expressive. The third house is associated with all forms of information, starting with basic talking/thinking and covering all forms of electronic transmission.

An interesting fact about the third house is that it covers relations with the community, neighbors, and siblings. This means that a sign located within this house in the natal charts will have decent relations throughout their lives. Handling such relationships is a pretty hefty task that comes naturally to Geminis, which also proves that they have been rightly placed in this house.

Another key thing to note about houses is that astrologers draw various conclusions when different planets transit through each house. So, if a planet transits through the third house, the signs associated with them receive integral information about their community/network. Usually, Geminis are born in such months that the alignment of the planets allows them to share the ruling traits of these two aspects — the houses and the planets/stars.

The next thing that anyone should know about zodiac signs is their association with the four basic elements. Throughout its development, scholars have associated zodiac signs with fire, water, air, and earth. Interpreters can yield better predictions since the relationships with these elements can have parallels to the exchanges between the signs associated with them. For example, the earth needs water to thrive (nourishment for growth), and water naturally exists on the earth, so water and earth signs can typically be good soulmates. Aries, Leo, and Sagittarius are considered fire signs, while Taurus, Virgo, and Capricorn are earth signs. Similarly, Gemini, Libra, and Aquarius are air signs, and Cancer, Scorpio, and Pisces are water signs. There are a lot of complicated interpretations of these elemental categories (triplicities) that take into account planets and the different signs but explaining that can be very cumbersome and is better left to an astrologer. What we need to concern ourselves is with the implications of Gemini being an "air" sign.

These four components are very relevant to this study as their combinations effectively create the world around us. So, it is up to us to recognize the type of energy that each of these elements demonstrates to better understand the output of their combinations. Each element comes together to shape a sign and its natural traits, enabling the sign bearer to be who he/she is. This elemental interpretation adds another layer of complexity to our topic, and piece-by-piece, we will eventually unravel the entire onion! The intricacy that is added allows astrologers to conceive a more complex and accurate chart, which leads to realistic predictions.

Air is usually deemed to be the element of intellectual people, as they seem to thrive on mental connections. All air signs are good at communicating, and they also deal reasonably well with others' arguments. The outlook on everything is changed when viewed through an air-sign bearer's eyes since their analysis is usually unique, and their thought process is also very special. The particular quality of an air-sign bearer is their ability to be empathetic. They can understand another person's pain and hardship if they focus on a case for long, and they might do just that since they are also highly curious individuals.

In general, the air means the surrounding space, and it is very important for human survival. Just like that, wisdom is vital for the spirit to thrive, and air bearers are known to be knowledge bearers. This is a vital trait for air signs due to the analytical nature of their thinking. It does not mean that they are smarter than everybody else around them, but they are more well-rounded than others because of their mental ability to process everything around them at a much faster rate. Their capacity to listen and reason plays a huge part in being well-rounded, allowing them to become a good communicator as well (PeacefulMind.com, n.d.).

The negative aspect of this sign is the self-evaluation that accompanies the mentally- inclined nature of these individuals. They tend to evaluate themselves more harshly than they do the world. This is probably a positive thing in many cases, but in others can be demoralizing... but the slumps in life are commonly followed by good times, and this self-evaluation is bound to bring better results sooner rather than later for air signs. Air signs also have a specific standard for themselves that they will go above and beyond to meet every time. This is usually associated with staying clean, maintaining their hygiene, and meeting a certain job performance model, among other things. This egoistic nature makes them excel in particular parts of their lives, but it can be tiresome in other parts.

Air signs are usually empathetic, as discussed, but are known to hold a grudge if angered to a certain extent. They are also prone to physical violence at times since their anger is not forgotten, unlike the fire sign's rage, but one thing to note here is that it is very hard to tick them off, and so if you did anger them, then you are probably wrong! The grudge may disappear almost immediately if you try to work things out with them because of their empathetic nature and their ability to listen to others. The air signs have been associated with blue, white, and yellow colors and have a liking for specific stones. Gemstones are the next important talking point about Geminis.

Gemstones are a very integral part of zodiac theory since they help in unlocking certain "powers". They are like birthstones but have been branded by astrology as being associated with the Sun signs. Each sign has one or two gemstones that can help in certain aspects of their lives. Gems are known to have protective and healing powers that compel a lot of people to keep them in their houses or with them at all times. A few also believe them to be lucky for them and can be very superstitious about their gemstones!

For the Gemini sign, the agate and the pearl are two very common stones. They represent the colors that the air signs have been associated with and are a reflection of their persona. The mentally active Gemini can benefit from the grounding essence of their stones. They can be reminded of being calm and can get through very tough situations if they use this stone as an ornament that they keep close to themselves at all times. This is also known to be a spiritual protector and can help from energy drains and eliminate stress. It has a divine aura that can aid in mental stimulation as well as decision-making. Many Geminis are very particular about their agate and pearl ornaments and carry them everywhere to support themselves with tough decisions (Melorra, 2020).

Now that all of all the zodiac interpretations key elements are covered, you will have a sense of where these predictions come from. This is key to understanding yourself and the sign that you are associated with in a more profound manner. These interpretations can be used to comprehend all the other chapters that follow, since they will focus on Gemini's personality traits and relationships. These explanations are also very useful for figuring out other signs like the Aquarius sign, since both of these signs lie in the air region. This guide's method of explanation is from "bottom to top" rather than being a top-down description. This means that the concepts are explained first, and then the big picture is drawn in the end. We find this way to be much more intriguing since all the views explained in this introduction are key to the explanations in the following chapters.

Different Gemini Profiles

It would be useless to just tell you about the zodiac signs' basic traits without a proper explanation since that information can be found anywhere on the Internet. This guide divides a person's life into many aspects/periods so that it is easier to explain the traits of this Sun sign. Another advantage of this unique style is that it allows greater readability and navigation through the guide. This means that you, as a reader, can go to any chapter and look for the relevant information in a tireless manner. It also makes it much more relatable and interactive. This session gives a brief introduction to each of the different profiles that the following chapters explain so that you know which one you can categorize yourself into.

The basic Gemini temperament is always active in all life stages, whether you know about it or not. This is something that more people need awareness about, and so is presented as the first chapter of this guide. It explains the basic and most evident "strengths and weaknesses" of the Gemini personality trait. It can be associated with all ages and every Gemini in any stage of his/her life.

Children are different from adults since they have virtually no responsibilities and a unique outlook on life. Many of the key traits that Geminis show in their early life result from their inquisitiveness. This might be the first sign that the child is following a set Gemini path, which leads to an overall balanced identity in the future. Adults should let them harness this personality, as they will grow into their mentally curious and analytical selves in a few years.

Geminis at work operate differently, so this is also a profile to analyze. This can be true for everyone since we all behave differently in different social surroundings. They have a unique skill set that is essential to excelling at many jobs, and so Geminis can be observed engaging in analytical debates and problem-solving their way through tough social situations as well as carrying out the job itself. They can form strictly professional relationships and enjoy their work at the same time. They work with excellent conviction, and their analytical skills help maintain their interest in their tasks. This is a very interesting profile that is associated with many working Geminis and can be accessed in the fifth chapter of this guide.

Geminis at other social gatherings behave in a very different way than when they are at work. This profile is perhaps the most talked-about profile by many astrologers when predicting their horoscope. At events and parties, they are always engaged in fun, humorous, and engaging debates since they are the Masters of Communication. Their spirit thrives on this activity and is constantly forcing the Gemini bearers to earn new people's trust. This allows them to make friends more easily than the other signs. This interesting analysis is discussed in more detail under the heading of the fourth chapter.

When in love they also present a compelling case. Their dual nature can be observed frequently in relationships, and can be the cause of their undoing. At the same time, it can also prove to be the main factor in keeping the relationship working. They are unique people, and so their love life is as complicated as it is unique.

Within the safe spaces of their homes, Geminis are also pretty different from any of the other profiles we discussed. Since they have higher mental prowess than other people, they can get bored quickly. So, while at home, they are always looking for something to occupy their time. They can also lose interest in their tasks because of the very dominant duality trait.

A few of the most popular Gemini celebrities are Sir Ian McKellen (most famous for playing Gandalf), Octavia Spencer, Amy Schumer, Tom Holland, Heidi Klum, Angelina Jolie, and Michael Cera. People who follow them can recognize key Gemini traits in their behavior after going through this guide!

Chapter 1: A Quick Primer – Suns, Moons, and Houses

Astrology is one of the world's oldest languages, using zodiac signs, planets, and houses to create your birth chart. This chart maps where the stars, sun, moon, and planets were at the time and place you were born. If you ever wondered why the full moon had a strange effect on you, this is why.

There are three primary points in your birth chart, mapping your personality – the sun, the moon, and rising. We all know our sun sign, but few of us are aware of our moon and rising signs. Understanding what all this means can influence everything you do in life.

All three – the sun, the moon, and the rising sign – are all in one particular zodiac sign on your chart. Each zodiac sign is in an elemental group – water, earth, air, or fire – and has a quality associated with it – cardinal, mutable, or fixed. Each also has one planetary ruler.

The Sun Sign

The sun provides your identity, what you shine out to everyone. It is the force that drives you on to be the best you can be. It represents your life experiences and your individuality, the energy type needed to help revitalize you, and how you recharge your batteries.

If your sun sign is one of the air signs – Libra, Gemini, or Aquarius – you express yourself intellectually and use social settings to recharge and revitalize yourself.

If your sun sign is one of the fire signs – Aires, Sagittarius, or Leo – aspiration and inspiration motivate you, and you use physical activity to revitalize yourself, along with pursuing specific life goals.

If your sun sign is one of the earth signs – Virgo, Taurus, or Capricorn – practicality and materialism motivate you. You revitalize yourself through productivity, heightening your senses, and working in the physical, not spiritual, world.

If your sun sign is one of the water signs – Pisces, Scorpio, or Cancer – emotional desire motivates you, and emotional experience and intimacy with people revitalize you.

The Moon Sign

Your moon sign represents your identity's soul, the subconscious part that nobody sees. This is the part of you that drives your emotions and helps you feel pain, pleasure, sorrow, and joy. It helps you understand how and why you react the way you do in emotional situations.

If your moon sign is one of the air signs – Libra, Gemini, or Aquarius – it represents how you react to change and evaluate it objectively. Social interaction helps you align with your inner self, as it does when you express ideas.

If your moon sign is one of the fire signs – Aires, Sagittarius, or Leo – you use direct action to react to change. When you express confidence, turn your back on negative self-talking, and show your strength, you align perfectly with your inner self.

If your moon sign is one of the earth signs – Virgo, Taurus, or Capricorn – you face change with stability and steadiness. Working towards your personal goals and being productive helps you to align with your inner self.

If your moon sign is one of the water signs – Pisces, Scorpio, or Cancer – you use emotion and sensitivity to face change. When you feel something deeply, you align with your inner self, but you must never forget to put self-love ahead of anything else.

The Rising Sign

Your rising sign is also called your Ascendant sign, and it represents your personality socially. It relates to whatever zodiac or sun sign was rising over the Eastern horizon at the time of your birth. It represents your physical body, the style you present to the world. It is a combination, a manifestation if you like, of your outer and inner world, helping you understand your approach to life and the type of energy your physical body needs.

If your rising sign is one of the air signs – Libra, Gemini, or Aquarius – you are friendly, curious, mentally quick off the mark, and you like to talk. Your approach to life is often in line with wanting to understand everything and everyone you meet.

If your rising sign is one of the fire signs – Aires, Sagittarius, or Leo – you are an active person, blunt, confident and to the point. You have a lot of physical energy and use it to your advantage to make your mark.

If your rising sign is one of the earth signs – Virgo, Taurus, or Capricorn – your focus is mainly on the physical world, and you are matter-of-fact. Your approach to life is steadfast, and that helps ground other people, especially when life is stressful.

If your rising sign is one of the water signs – Pisces, Scorpio, or Cancer – you are empathetic and sensitive; your environment has a direct influence on you. Your approach to life is an emotional and deep one.

The Twelve Houses

When planets visit any of the houses, that part of your chart will light up, adding energy to the specific House's traits. Astrologers use these houses to predict the areas in your life that will come into focus, allowing you to determine the best course of action at that time.

Houses 1-to-6 are the personal houses, while the last six are the interpersonal houses.

• 1st House – The start of the zodiac, the very first of everything, including self, impressions and appearance, fresh starts, leadership initiative, and new beginnings. Ruled by Aries, the sign on the 1st House cusp is your ascendent or rising sign.

• 2nd House – Relates to your physical and material environment, including your senses – touch, taste, smell, sound, and sight. It is ruled by Taurus and is responsible for self-esteem, money, and income.

• 3rd House – Rules communication, including gadgets, talking, devices like cell phones, and thinking. Ruled by Gemini, it covers community affairs, travel, schools, communication, libraries, your neighborhood, and siblings.

• 4th House – Ruled by Cancer, this House lies at the bottom of the wheel and is responsible for foundations, including your privacy, home, parents (especially your mother), security, children, TLC, and nurturing.

• 5th House – Ruled by Leo, this House is responsible for self-expression, color, drama, fun, romance, attention, and play.

• 6th House – Responsible for health and service, including organization, schedules, fitness, nutrition, exercise, healthy living, and routines. Ruled by Virgo, it also covers your helpfulness and what you do for others.

- 7th House – This House is responsible for people and relationships. Ruled by Libra, it covers professional and personal relationships, matters associated with those relationships, marriage, contracts, and business dealings.

- 8th House – One of the more mysterious houses, this one rules sex, birth, death, mysteries, transformation, the merging of energies, and deep bonding. Ruled by Scorpio, it rules property, money, inheritance, real estate, and investments.

- 9th House – This House rules long-distance and international travel, the higher mind, inspiration, foreign languages, optimism, expansion, broadcasting, publishing, and higher education. Ruled by Sagittarius, it also covers religion, gambling, risk-taking, luck, adventure, ethics, and morals.

- 10th House – The topmost House on the wheel and the most public, this House rules incorporation, public image, structures, tradition, honors, fame, awards and achievements, rules, authority, discipline, and fatherhood. Ruled by Capricorn, the cusp is also known as the Midheaven, giving astrologers an idea about your career path in life.

- 11th House – This House is responsible for groups, friendship, teams, technology, society, electronic media, social justice, networking, rebellion, and humanitarian causes. Ruled by Aquarius, it also governs eccentricity, originality, surprises, sudden events, astronomy, invention, and science fiction.

- 12th House – The final House governs endings, like the last stages of any project, loose ends, the afterlife, completions, surrender, and old age. Ruled by Pisces, it also governs separation, hospitals, institutions, hidden agendas, jails, secret enemies, the subconscious mind, creativity, film, arts, journals, and poetry.

Chapter 2: Gemini Strengths and Weaknesses

Like any other human, Geminis excel in several aspects of life while struggling in others. Significant research and studies have highlighted certain personality traits attributed to Geminis. The best part is that Geminis can now know and understand them using this guide.

Strengths

Geminis are often gregarious and sociable human beings. They are enthusiastic about social gatherings and excited to meet and talk to new people, but this does not mean that they are annoyingly chatty. If you have a friend who is a Gemini, notice what piques their interest. They are likely keen on deep things in life or any specialized discipline, and that is what they love discussing with their peers.

But this does not imply that Geminis cannot talk about anything else. They thrive in conversations and love giving their two cents' worth on everything. This quality gives them an edge in small yet crucial everyday discussions. For example, Geminis find it relatively easy when journeying through high school and college. Making friends or interacting with the institution's hierarchy comes easily to young Geminis.

If you are a Gemini, you probably love parties and parades. If you ever host a party, make sure to have Geminis on your guest list – they will make the best out of anything. Their excellent conversational skills allow them to hold a crowd and make every person in the room feel welcome. With exceptional interpersonal skills come brilliant flirting skills as well. Geminis flourish on dates. If you go on a date with a Gemini, you will notice how hard they try to make you feel comfortable. They make sure you have fun-filled experiences while simultaneously enjoying themselves. A date with a Gemini is bound to be a heartwarming day, but more on that later.

Along with being a brilliant conversationalist, a Gemini uses their outgoing nature to be friendly with others. Rather than being cocky when conversing, Geminis are gracious and kind with whomever they interact with. No matter how enthusiastic they may be, they care about the perspectives of those on the other side of the table. They can have themselves heard along with hearing out others. This trait makes Geminis perfect pacifiers or moderators.

They like to mediate conversations and try their best to accommodate each and every person sitting with them. Need someone to break the ice between you and your crush? Ask your Gemini friend to be your wingman. Are you too shy to strike up a conversation with a group across the court? Ask your Gemini friend to join you for the day. Want to clarify a misunderstanding between yourself and a loved one? A Gemini should be able to patch up the two of you. With a Gemini, you are highly unlikely to feel left out in a conversation.

Besides being loquacious, Geminis are more than often exceptionally energetic and zestful people to have around. They not only know to talk with enthusiasm, but they also physically express their excitement about things they deeply care about. Their body language gives them away and describes the notions they have in mind. This makes Geminis very jovial people to be around. They may perform impersonations of someone or tell a story by acting a few parts of it to make it look hilarious. No one makes more of the day than a Gemini does. They detest boredom and tend to keep themselves actively busy, either by doing productive work or killing time with close friends. Their huge tank of energy helps them to be active and social. They take a long time to tire themselves out and retire to their beds. Look around in your social circle and see which people are the liveliest of them all. See how many Geminis you find.

Another positive trait Geminis possess is the ability to stay optimistic. Geminis tend to find happiness in the smallest of events that take place during the day. They hope for the best and do not waste time worrying about what fate holds for them. Geminis always live in the moment. They are likely to be happy all the time unless something serious comes up. They do their best to keep themselves, and everyone around them, full of joy and optimism all the time.

If you have a Gemini friend, you may have noticed that they are very cheerful and oddly optimistic about things in life. They do not give in to petty unfortunate events, like a lousy exam or a small car crash, and let it ruin their day. Geminis live their lives to the fullest. They wake up every day as an adventurer and go to sleep hoping to enjoy the next day as well. Their optimistic attitude also makes them excellent sympathizers. A Gemini can uplift those who feel low and help them regain their confidence; they always inspire other people to be happy and positive. If you have been facing a lot of stress lately, ask your Gemini friend for help. They will graciously help if they can.

One of the better strengths a Gemini can benefit from is adjusting and adapting to situations quickly. Gemini is always craving new ventures. They are comfortable taking on new things every other minute. They are capable of shifting their attitude and adjusting it to the situation at hand. If you are a Gemini, ask your loved ones to rate your improvisational skills. There is a good chance of you scoring a solid nine out of ten. Notice how your Gemini friends respond to sudden changes in activities around them. It is like having a supercomputer's speed in reacting to scenarios, and this is not an overstatement. Even in life-changing yet gradual transitions, they quickly process it in their head and adjust to the flow. Recently shifted to a new house or city with a Gemini sibling or parent? Notice how they adapt to their new home within a week. If your Gemini son or daughter just joined college, you need not worry. As long as you keep in touch, they will thrive there.

The same applies to spontaneous plans and gatherings. Most Geminis are explorers and want to try everything at least once. The word "no" just does not seem to be in their dictionary. They like planning spontaneous adventures and trips and will tag along on short notice. They make time for joyful occasions, and that is what makes them such good friends, colleagues, and team members. Working late at night on a deadline at the office with a Gemini? Ask them to join you on a drive around the block. Chances are they might respond with a better crazy idea for spending the next few minutes. Reminisce on any sudden plans you were a part of. Was it a Gemini friend who came up with the idea in the first place?

The fact that Gemini is able to contribute to any discussion indicates their intelligence. Any person who can talk with you for hours on a diverse set of topics and be kind and considerate while doing so is bound to possess a remarkable intellect. Usually, these people are Gemini. Besides being companionable, they are known and observed to have an inquisitive mind. They like learning more about almost everything.

As mentioned earlier, Geminis despise getting bored. This is the reason why they welcome new ideas and intriguing knowledge with both arms. It is easy to find Gemini engrossed in books or seated in seminars that others generally avoid. Did you just read a new book and have no one to talk about it? Mention it to a Gemini, and they will get back to you with their critical insights. Gemini students tend to ask fascinating questions. That is the reason teachers and professors are likely to develop a liking for Gemini students. On the downside, they might be judged as know-it-alls to their peers, but it might be the same with academic exams.

A Gemini prefers intellectual understanding over ideals. If you are a Gemini, you may find it hard to accept something until you have seen the proof. You tend to not care about noisy news on the television. Instead, you seek credible sources for your research and try to understand each aspect before accepting it. Even once you do learn something new, you crave updates and further insights on the matter. This intuition fortifies you against rumors and fake claims. The beauty of being a Gemini that it is highly unlikely for you to be wrong, or at least ill-informed.

Being clever with a lovely sense of humor is another one of the many perks of being a Gemini. When with friends, they like partaking in banter a lot. Belonging to an "air" sign, they are generally empathetic people with a long fuse. Instead of being sensitive about it, a Gemini may reply with a snarky comment. No matter how hard you hit them, they avoid being triggered and outraged right away. They do keep a count of what is happening, but not in the form of a grudge.

While history shows us many great Gemini thinkers, like Blaise Pascal, intelligence does not necessarily refer to great thinkers. Gemini is quick in finding solutions to everyday problems. They do stunningly in situations that require immediate answers. They do not need to know the laws of matter and motion to escape hectic traffic. Similarly, they know how to react to urgent moments in sports like football, squash, badminton, etc. Notice how good your Gemini friends are at riddles. Being Gemini allows you to breeze through daily challenges that other people might surrender to.

Intelligence combined with proficient speaking skills and an improvisational attitude makes for a lethal asset for Geminis. They can think quickly on their feet and react well to situations. You may call them "quick thinkers" as they are able to make informed, rational choices in a short period. If you are a Gemini, you will be sought after the most when building a team, as you have the social and intellectual skills to be a crucial team member. The team is most likely to revolve around a Gemini as well.

Weaknesses

While Geminis flourish in several aspects of life, they do have a few shortcomings. As you may notice, most of these flaws are just the flip side of the benefits that being a Gemini brings. Not all Geminis must have each one of these defects. It depends on how they live their lives and tackle these weaknesses. This book will also highlight a few tips other Gemini use to overcome these mere limitations. They might or might not work for you.

While Geminis may appear to converse with a group of people benevolently, their habit of accommodating everyone might make them look two-faced. At one point, they might favor any issue, while at another point they might completely disagree with the same proposition. By embracing a set different of opinions, Geminis might end up being dishonest to themselves. They tend to mix up their own beliefs while conceding other people's thoughts. This process confuses many fellow Geminis and throws them into a spiral of self-doubts. So, one weakness a Gemini may struggle to deal with is bewilderment regarding themselves. Look around at your Gemini peers. Have you noticed them having multiple opinions or contradicting insights on any topic?

The next two problems we will be discussing stem from the weakness mentioned above. While Geminis might have a hard time figuring out what they really stand for, they also deal with nervousness when making crucial life-changing decisions. With doubt in one's own beliefs comes doubt in one's actions. If you are a Gemini, you may notice that you are indecisive at times. For instance, we discussed that most Geminis easily adjust to a new home, but the process of selecting the house is not a Gemini's cup of tea. They tend to be critical about the smallest details, so much so that they build hundreds and thousands of choices in their heads. Selecting or choosing is the worst situation for a Gemini.

Ever been to a shopping mall with a Gemini? Just give them a set of clothes to choose from and see how long they take to pick their favorite. In their head, they might be thinking of many things; the latest trend, a magazine or actor they saw, a friend's suggestion, the price, the number of times they might wear that clothing or only what they already have in their wardrobe. While it may make sense to make informed and calculated discussions, scrutinizing every single thing tires them out. It is better if you do not ask a Gemini for a choice of movies on movie night. They might fuss over it unnecessarily, ultimately watching whatever the majority decides. This is the reason they love going with the flow and tagging along in events.

Another negative trait attributed to Geminis is their fondness for materialistic gain. Gemini people are usually shortsighted when it comes to identifying the inner beauty of someone. They are dazzled by the fineness and grandeur of the world. They want the same class and beauty that impresses them for themselves as well. While it is common for anyone to be attracted to charm and intelligence, Gemini tends to overlook the hidden yet meaningful aspects of things, people, and places. Understandably, they may try to associate themselves with rich and attractive people and end up getting disappointed.

While most Gemini makes very good friends, a Gemini might ditch their close friends for someone with a lot of charm and beauty. This can be detrimental to not only the maturity of Geminis but also their social life. They are likely to lose friendships like this and may end up having fewer shoulders to cry on. The worst part about this is that Gemini is likely to repeat this mistake and spiral down into the dark abyss. Just as they find happiness in little things in life, Gemini should also embrace people for who they are rather than what they outwardly look like – a lesson most Geminis learn the hard way. Did you recently go through a broken friendship? Was it a Gemini? If so, what do you think were the reasons?

Belonging to the element of Air, Geminis usually fail to connect their thoughts with reality. Geminis happen to be people who believe more in theories rather than actual practice. They may appear to be idealists who believe anything is possible. They are mostly driven by sheer will. While the raw will is good for people lacking motivation like Geminis, it blinds them from the practicality of their thoughts and opinions. This may also be seen when Gemini requires something they do not need. They seem to face a "disconnection between introspection and actuality" when making decisions (preparingforpeace.org, 2020). This can easily be noticed when Gemini is confronted with blame for something they did not do. Even though parts of them may be puzzled regarding what wrong they may have done, they are likely to apologize since it is the nobler thing to do. You can do a short experiment on your Gemini friend to see this. Try blaming your Gemini friend for losing something you gave him/her. How do they react? This trait can play heavily in circumstances with higher stakes. To fix this, we recommend Gemini friends develop assertiveness and awareness of their immediate surroundings.

Since Geminis are usually hungry for knowledge, they are prone to impulsive thinking. For instance, a Gemini hears a different opinion or theory about something; they are likely to change their own perceptions due to that influence. We do not mean to imply that Geminis do not think for themselves. Instead, they get, once again, easily puzzled when shown a set of opinions or thoughts. If they do not discover the truth through their research, they fall prey to bewilderment. In the worst-case scenario, this could lead to reckless decision-making after wholeheartedly believing and changing their thoughts on a topic. This impulsive reactionary behavior may also stand in the way of their accomplishing long-term goals. They may feel motivated for a certain task one day but might leave it hanging the next. For this very reason, Gemini struggles to deal with casual, gossipy rumors. It may not be right to ask the person themselves, and any other source they may listen to will only add to the list of stories they heard. While Gemini is stunning in conversations head-on, they hate these sorts of "Chinese whispers." Notice this amongst your Gemini peers. How indecisive do you think are they?

The same impulsive attitude may apply to emotional behavior. While Gemini may have a high temperament, they are likely to burst out in front of anyone once they reach their limit. They remember what was said and meant, pile it up in memory, and execute a reactionary response once overload reaches its limit. Gemini may greet you with a bright smile like an angel or yell at you with a horrifying expression like a devil. This may lead to many Geminis to go through breakups or broken friendships. They may end up being aggressive to a colleague and ruin their relationship with them forever. Any Gemini should work on their emotions if they tend to do this a lot. Since they are likely to react quickly, it is also likely that a Gemini might say something wrong or hurtful. To regulate this behavior can be extremely stressful for Geminis, especially if they do this more regularly. While Geminis should try to control their impulsiveness, other peers belonging to other signs should learn to cut them a bit of slack wherever possible. Are you a Gemini going through similar circumstances? Try explaining it to your loved ones and ask them for help.

If you are a Gemini, you may find it challenging to sustain your motivation when working on a month-long project. This may because you experience a change in priorities or may simply get bored. If your school hours consist of long raw lectures with barely any extra-curricular activities, you may not enjoy school as a Gemini. Geminis do not thrive in routines, especially when the activities are restricted, boring, and repetitive. They barely have any fixed routine and tend to go along with whatever life throws at them. This makes Geminis blind to the big picture in life, relationships, friendships, and careers. The requirement to always keep themselves entertained and engaged is a Gemini's biggest weakness. Since they like delving into multiple topics of their interest, they may pile a lot of stuff on their shoulders, more than they can carry. If you are a Gemini, you might want to keep track of all the commitments you make and when delivery is expected. Losing track of time is easy for anyone, especially a Gemini. They may sacrifice hours to procrastination, only to fulfill their hunger for amusement. Being a good friend, you should try to keep tabs on your Gemini friends and help them see the big picture.

Gemini is curious and craves knowledge about everything they can think of. While being a seeker of knowledge may be a charming quality to possess, many Geminis take it a step too far by getting deeply interested in other people's lives. They might want to be continuously updated about events and changes in everyone's lives. This behavior can rightly annoy anyone they converse with. They may worsen a person's mental health if they ask a bad question and unknowingly attack their insecurities.

Have a small scar on your cheek? A Gemini will be sure to ask you about it and the story behind it. Just came home from the dentist? Your Gemini sibling will want to know all that happened. Went on a date recently? Your Gemini neighbor will ask you every single detail. If you have a Gemini friend, notice how much they may encourage you to share your secrets. Even though this may help them build friendships, most people may find Geminis nosy due to this trait. Geminis, being the conversationalists they are, might appear to be intruding when interacting with new people. Not everyone they meet will want to answer questions like where they live, how many boyfriends they have had, or how their childhood was. If you are a Gemini, start observing caution when asking questions and talking. What is your question about? Think of any way your question may hurt the person.

While Gemini may be kind and empathetic, they are usually undependable. Their indecisiveness takes a toll on them, and they tend to become irresponsible with the task at hand. This is why Gemini is less sought after when seeking advice. No matter how religiously they may have committed initially, many Geminis fail to get the job done. They pile up too much work, not knowing when to stop. Ultimately, they leave most of it incomplete and miss their deadlines. Normally, a person will rely on someone who is specialized in the field, committed to the work, confident, and self-aware. The fact that many Gemini find trouble while evaluating themselves make it difficult to rely on them. A Gemini may get bored when preparing a tedious long Excel sheet. The next thing you know, they spent the rest of the day on Netflix or shopping. If you send an invitation to a Gemini of an event way before the day, they will probably cancel it as the day closes in. It is not like Geminis are rude or arrogant. It is sheer irresponsibility that stems from their inherited characteristics and leads them astray. If you are a Gemini going through the same situation, we recommend making to-do lists and limiting the tasks you commit to. While Gemini might have a hard time helping others with work, they will not let anyone down for a fun night out.

As we discussed earlier, Geminis are judged as having many personalities. People may judge them as two-faced or people-pleasers. Even in astrology, Gemini represents "duality". It is not really a Gemini's fault here. They may only be trying to accommodate and be friendly to people. The problem lies in when they overdo it and accidentally make others uncomfortable. Judging by how indecisive Gemini people can be, they might be visualized as people with unstable personalities.

We discussed how Geminis struggle to find what they actually stand for. They may fret in their head over contradictory opinions, unfair reactions, or differences in treatment for different people. For instance, a Gemini may profusely criticize their local government for mismanagement but when talking with someone in favor of the government, they might discuss other reasons for the incident and justify the government's efforts as sufficient. This two-faced behavior further adds to the unreliability of Geminis. Gemini can suffer excruciatingly from this flaw, as they are likely to lose friends, acquaintances, and clients.

Generally, Geminis are amazing and charming personalities. Their strengths enable them to get along with people quickly. But they tend to struggle in their social lives when they overdo their loquaciousness and unintentionally make others uncomfortable. Other negative traits are only the flip side of their strengths. Gemini should work hard to strike a balance between the two without giving up the type of person they essentially are.

Chapter 3: The Gemini Child

Children are the joy of people's lives; they remind them of how simple life was once, but kids are commonly misunderstood, which enables the adults around them to make uneducated decisions about their growth and needs. If you have Gemini children and want to understand a few of their actions, then you have come to the right place! This chapter will cover all the common traits and characteristics of Gemini children that adults can consider peculiar. The last section of this chapter aims to focus on the differences between young Gemini girls and boys. This is an important section as there are a few critical differences that not a lot of people are aware of. It can help you in understanding the young Gemini boy or girl in your life!

This chapter can also be an interesting read for young adult and adult Geminis that seek to reminisce about their childhood, since it will bring back all those memories that you thought you had forgotten! All the explanations below arise from the universal components of zodiac astrology that were discussed in the introduction of this guide (common elements were ruling planets, houses, natal charts, gemstones, and much more).

Common Traits of Gemini Children

The very first significant action in a child's life is talking. Mercury rules Geminis, so essentially, they become efficient communicators later on in life, but this ability to articulate begins early. Gemini children start talking (or mumbling words/gibberish) slightly earlier than other toddlers. Do not be afraid of this early action since Gemini children have this "expressive nature" discussed at the start of this guide. If you are a Gemini, then you should probably ask your parents about the time you first started talking. You'll probably hear that it was earlier than your siblings. Parents are recommended to encourage this behavior by performing activities (or using different forms of media, such as music) that are designed to bring out this expressive nature. If nurtured correctly, the children can then go on to inherit their ability of articulation!

This does not mean that if your child resides on the quieter side of the talking spectrum, there must be something wrong with him/her. A surprising amount of Gemini kids are on the quieter side, but they are quick-witted and charming when they need to be. This quick-wittedness also means that they have the ability to articulate efficiently since they are constantly in a dialogue with themselves. Even if they are not talkative all the same, you still have to stick with the same routine that was explained in the earlier paragraph. As parents, you have to surround your Gemini child with books, music, puzzles, and other such media that will allow them to keep on having their inner dialogue.

In both the cases explained above, the Gemini child is always expressing his curiosity in different forms. This means that along with being charming and quick-witted, the Gemini child is also very curious. This characteristic will evolve with time and will play a major role in the traits explained in the adult life profiles in the chapters that follow. Remember this when reading those chapters.

Another common trait that Gemini children have is their ever-changing interests in things. The duality concept that is clear in many Geminis in the world takes its roots from this stage in their lives. At this early stage, Geminis are very interested in examining, performing, and conducting new activities/things. It is often observed that they also shift from one activity to the next very quickly too. This means that Gemini children are often interested in a combination of different experiences rather than focusing on extracting maximum utility from just one experience. This also results in the kids getting bored much more quickly than other kids, since they want new activities so often.

Gemini parents have their work cut out for them since they always have to find new things for their kids to do. As a Gemini, you can understand this since you also probably did the same thing as a child. This results in adult Geminis also getting bored easily. With a lot of free time, Geminis will be always on the lookout for random chores and interesting projects to invest their time in. This trait also emerges from the curiosity characteristic discussed earlier.

These will be the first few signs of the dual-nature personality that your Gemini child will soon inherit, but one positive can be drawn out from this trait! Geminis that change their minds often are also known to be adaptable and great problem solvers since they are used to facing different situations.

There is also a negative from this dual-nature ability. Gemini children are so focused on diversifying their experience that it is hard to make them focus on one particular activity. This may hinder their ability to focus, and in turn, affect their abilities. We recommend parents allow them to experiment with different experiences, and as they get older, their minds will develop naturally. This natural development will allow them to live a satisfactory life since they will not be pressured to learn one craft; rather, they will have a combination of different experiences to boost their capabilities.

Gemini kids also start to crawl at a very early age because of their curious nature. To feed their curiosity and expressive nature, they often go into places that other babies will not go. Any Gemini parent should baby-proof their entire house, as once their child becomes an explorer, they will leave no space untouched. Parents are also advised to keep a close eye on their Gemini children for their safety. They need to be extra careful with a Gemini child since their curious nature can get them into dangerous spots around the house. This trait grants the baby more freedom to move around, but it also means that the baby will sometimes not like to be confined in small spaces. The Gemini child will find this restricting experience an obstacle to fulfilling their "mental" hunger. So, in many ways, parents of Gemini children should be relieved that they need not put a lot of effort into parenting since allowing the Gemini child to develop naturally is the best way forward!

All the traits above can be observed frequently in the home, but they can be translated into different traits when the Gemini child is at school. The school is one of the first places outside of the home that a child gets to experience, so it is fairly obvious that he/she will exhibit different traits there. The next few traits are often observed amongst Gemini children when they are at school.

The first common trait is the unpredictable nature of Gemini kids. Due to the dual and unpredictable nature of the children, they may do something that means trouble for them or someone else in the school, but it can also mean that many positive things are also possible because of this unpredictable nature. Due to this curious and unpredictable nature, it is difficult for a Gemini child to follow a strict schedule. This means the child might exhibit many negative behavioral traits. Since going to school is an activity that follows a strict schedule, the child may throw tantrums in classes or during other activities if they lose their interest and follow their free souls. Following a strict sleep routine is also important for going to school. Unfortunately, that too is tough to ask from a Gemini child because of this trait. All of these combined can create an uninterested individual that may be rebellious when they move into their teenage years.

All of this should not worry a parent because of the following traits that are quite positive for a school-going Gemini child. A Gemini Child is a very good socializer since they have an infectious and endless energy that can attract all sorts of people. They can thrive in social situations and activities in the school. This allows the children to be well-liked by their peers as well as the school staff. They are sure to reap the benefits of building a strong relationship with the community. This stems from Gemini's ruling house that is deeply associated with positive relationships with the community and Gemini's siblings. If these relationships last for a long time, they can positively or negatively impact the Gemini's life during their adult years.

The dual nature of the Gemini can make it difficult for children to choose. This can become an obstacle in situations like a verbal class activity or deciding their lunch in the cafeteria, but this can easily be navigated through with a little guidance. The Gemini child is very responsive, so adults will know immediately about their wants and needs. They can then use this information to offer them guidance.

These traits summarize the life that your Gemini child will follow inside your house as well as in their school. It is useful to know about these traits because the next part of this section will explain how you can use this information. The following paragraphs of this section will cover the basic needs of a Gemini child. As parents, you can offer an environment that encourages their growth by fulfilling their needs according to their zodiac sign. Gemini teens and adults can also read the next few paragraphs to learn a few tricks about how to navigate through their negative traits.

The most important thing that can be derived from all the above traits is that the Gemini child reacts positively to joyful interaction and mental stimulation. They always need to talk to someone or to be occupied in something that challenges their mental capabilities. If parents continuously talk to and make sounds at their children (positive interaction), the child will respond in positive sounds and broken words. As parents, you need to invest in good literature and fun activities (like puzzles and board games). Hopefully, these games will keep your child interested in them for a while before you need to think of something new and fun. This cycle of investment and interest should continue until the child automatically finds something that grabs their attention for longer than just a few weeks/days.

Parents also need to take care of their children in the sense that they always need to keep an eye on their curious movements as they may run into something dangerous. It is good to baby-proof the house because Gemini babies need this protection more than other types.

Most of all, a Gemini child needs a patient parent who can guide them through their toughest choices. Making choices can be a recurring challenge in their life, and if they have a stable influence to guide them through it, then they may grow up to be very well-rounded people that boast an array of experiences to boost their capabilities.

Differences Between Young Gemini Boys and Girls

There are a few personality differences that are dependent on the gender of the child. Astrologers claim that parents, as well as Geminis, need to understand such differences to better navigate through their lives. This section will give a short overview of those differences so that you can make well-informed decisions in the future.

The main difference between these two genders is their forms of communication. Now, this information might not be applicable to all the Geminis of the world but since it is frequently reported, it may be helpful. The male child has a different way of communicating than the girl, even though both of them are pretty expressive. The female child may address her curiosity by asking a lot of questions. When we say a lot, it might be an understatement. These questions will range from simple ones to very complex ones, which will require you to research them online, but the male child is always looking to put his quick wits to good use and is always up for a practical joke or two.

Both of them still retain their basic traits discussed earlier in the chapter but how they use them is a bit different. Another trait that is utilized differently is the duality aspect. Girls tend to shift their interests a lot more than boys. They may appear interested in something on one day while doing the opposite thing on the other. Boys are unpredictable, but they tend to stick to their interests more often than girls.

Another rare trait that is sometimes not found in Gemini girls is the ability to multitask efficiently. Gemini boys tend to multitask frequently in their teens and build up the ability so that they can access it in their adult life. Women have a natural tendency to multitask, but it is less frequently reported in Gemini girls than Gemini boys.

There are more differences but those can arise on a more individual basis rather than a collective basis. Thus, they were not included in this section. The differences that were selected are a common representation of a Gemini boy and a Gemini girl. Parents can use this information and link it with their children's needs to make better decisions about their wellbeing.

Chapter 4: The Gemini in Love

To trust a person and to offer your entire self to them can be a daunting task. So, falling in love with someone can prove to be difficult for certain people, as they struggle to open up. It is even more challenging for people to find themselves a perfect partner to marry. Finding someone who is perfectly compatible with your personality and will perfectly complement you is very difficult. Rarely do people find the right person that will not leave their side until the end of time.

Every person's personality traits are unique, and to find this person – someone with complementing characteristics – can be a hard task. Even if one finds the perfect person, they might struggle with various obstacles in the relationship. Be it a girlfriend and boyfriend or a husband and wife, everyone faces challenges in their relationships. Many manage to surpass these challenges, while other relationships are shattered due to the pressure of these obstacles. The key to the success behind a long-lasting marriage and a happy couple is the expectation of these hurdles. If people expect these challenges, they will be better prepared and have the ideal mindset to survive the issues and save their relationship. You might think that finding love and dodging these challenges might be a matter of luck. You are wrong. What if I tell you, finding love and holding on to it for a long time can become easy with the understanding of your horoscope and your birth chart? No, I am not kidding. Your star sign describes what kind of personality you have inherited, and if one is aware of these traits, they can find their perfect partner with comparable ease.

So, if you have a crush on a Gemini in your neighborhood, college, or workplace and want to discover the right way to pursue it, then you have found the right book. Similarly, if you are in a happy relationship with a Gemini and want to know any obstacles that you need to be cautious about, this book is perfect for you too. In this chapter, we will explore the compatibility of a Gem with other star signs. We will learn about how the personalities can clash or contrast and how they can start their exploratory journey of finding their first love. We will focus mainly on Gemini's attributes and tips that will help you date a Gemini. It will also cater to a Gemini by looking at various topics from their perspective. It will serve as a place for a Gemini to understand their habitual reactions to love and provide a guide for them to navigate a healthy relationship.

When you are a teenager, you have a lot of emotions and have inherited expectations from the people around you. When it comes to love, a teenager finds it difficult to navigate this relationship and find the starting point to go about it. Expectations, fears, or excitement often blur their thoughts. As explained before, Geminis have dual personalities, and searching for love can be difficult for a teen Gemini. They can be confused by the dual personalities that might guide them in opposite directions. This section will help a Gemini, especially a teen, understand love and be aware of the expectations to carry.

First, let's emphasize Gemini's dual personality trait and how it impacts their love life. Imagine being on a night out, dancing carelessly, and having the best time of your life. You have your friends around, and you are the most comfortable that you can get. A stranger comes up to you, and you both start talking. As a Gemini, you like conversations and are very easy to talk to. When you get back home, you think of going out on a date with this person. A Gemini can feel they are too young for it, or even if they go out on a date, they might not pursue it further. The thought of love can frighten a few young Geminis, as they think it will shackle their freedom, but a Gemini needs to realize their dual personality and that a decade down the lane, they might feel that they are too old for love. Anyway, a Gemini will never think that it is the correct time to explore their love options. They will either be too young, too old, too busy, or too free to get involved in a relationship. A Gemini, especially a teen, needs to realize that there is no time for love – it is timeless.

There is not an age bracket for finding true love. Fearing that love will restrict their freedom is not the right thought process for a Gemini. Despite being great lovers, Gems distance themselves from commitment even if it's what they desire. They love adventures and exploring different interests. There is no organization in their life as they strive for spontaneous thrills. So, it is important that Geminis keep this in mind because the fear of losing time and freedom can cause them to miss out on the right person. Just make the leap when you find someone you love unconditionally and who respects your interests and personality. The kind of people who will gel well with you and be compatible with your complex personality is explored in the next section.

Second, as we briefly talked about before, most people are buried in expectations when it comes to the topic of love. Having expectations is human nature and something that everyone does, but the Geminis are some, if not the only, people who doubt the expectations they have. Being so energetic and social, they think it is difficult to find someone who can mirror their zeal for adventure and travel. They also doubt that anyone can match their intellectual capacity, their desire for funny, entertaining conversations and intellectual, witty conversations other times.

Young Geminis need to be assured that there is someone who can and will match their love for adventures and fulfill the needs of their dual personalities, but expectations can limit your experience; in this case, never settle for less. Gems need to be constantly in search of the right person and persevere until it happens. Note that this does not mean that you look for someone who is perfect or a perfect clone of the perfect person that you have imagined. Instead, look out for those who just fulfill your emotional, spiritual, intellectual, and physical needs. Keeping this in mind will allow you to make the right decisions that you do not regret in the future.

Now that we have highlighted the two most significant things that can often spoil the experience of finding love for a Gemini. Let's approach this topic from the perspective of an outsider trying to impress a Gemini.

First, try to talk about something they might not know. Geminis are very inquisitive people and crave learning. Talking about your dreams, hobbies, and passions, especially something that they do not know about, will excite them and make them more interested in you. Your uniqueness will attract the Gemini's attention and will cause them to come back for more, as there is a possibility that there is more that they can learn from you. Also, it is essential that you are original. Do not repeat yourself or copy the same old trick. Geminis tend to get bored easily, so treat every chance that you have as your last chance.

Second, Geminis like to struggle. Try to act disinterested in the Gemini, and they will work to earn your attention. This might annoy them initially, but it can allow you to strengthen your bond in the long run. It will also make them appreciate you in the relationship more. Play this move cleverly because overdoing it can cause them to repel from you.

Last, try to make a Gemini feel comfortable in his or her own skin. Geminis are mutable, which means that they can change with time or change with the flow of the situation. This was touched upon before and is also evident through their symbols, which means "twins". Rather than restricting them from exhibiting their various personalities, allow them to remold themselves at their own convenience. This will make them feel comfortable with you, as they can put their true self at the show. Moreover, if you can be spontaneous with plans and trips, it will make Geminis happy and can leave a good impression on them.

These are a few of the significant things that Geminis need to consider when exploring love and non-Geminis when trying to pursue one.

Now that we have touched upon these things that will make your journey of finding love a little smoother let's talk about things from the other perspective. We will cover how to react from the perspective of someone who is in a relationship with a Gemini. The next section will equip them with ideas about how to respond in the relationship. In the next section, we will discover a Gemini's compatibility with the rest of the zodiac signs. We will explore the relationship in a manner that can cater to both Gemini and other zodiac signs. Be mindful that these are the traits that only their sun suggests, but a conscientious effort from both parties can alter any differences.

A Quick Guide to Dating a Gemini

The previous part of this chapter has explored different techniques when trying to engage in a relationship with a Gemini, but things take a different turn when you find yourself in one. You might encounter situations that you have not been in before and might find yourself exposed to aspects of your partner's personality that you have never seen before. In these scenarios, one needs to know how to react and tend to their partner's needs. To make a relationship last, it is vital that you understand your partner and act appropriately towards their needs.

This section will list a few pointers that can come in handy for someone in a relationship with a Gemini.

Listen to Your Partner

Geminis love to talk endlessly. It is a significant part of their personality, and they are curious to know more about things. Do not burden yourself with thinking of a topic for discussion; instead, let the Gemini take the lead, because they will have various topics in mind to chat about. Just be careful not to interrupt the Gemini during this conversation because they might think that you are not interested.

Be Patient with Your Partner

When going into a relationship with a Gemini, you should expect that their moods and behavior might change regularly. They can be fun and happy one moment and can get angry and grumpy the next. In these situations, you should not allow their behavior to get to you. Refrain from taking it personally and try talking to them, inquiring about what is bothering them.

Do Not Force Gemini's to Make a Decision

Duality nature once again presents itself here. Due to this personality trait, a Gemini might be stuck in confusion over two available choices. One part might want the first choice, while the other part of their personality might be inclined to pursue the second option. Confusion between having Indian or Thai food on a date night can be one of these situations. If you find yourself in a similar situation, then do not force your choice on them. Gemini hates it. Instead, you can approach such problems by making a suggestion. Note that even if you frame your preference so that it comes across as a preference rather than a decision, it will allow you to dodge any arguments. So, instead of forcing them to have Indian, you can rephrase it and say, "We had Thai last night, and I heard there is a new Indian restaurant that has opened down the street. Should we try something new today?"

Never Break the Trust of a Gemini

Geminis are very loving and enjoy the company of humans. So, it makes a lot of sense that they invest a lot of their trust in their friends and partners. After you have broken their trust, Geminis might forgive you and accept you back into their life, but you will never be able to regain their trust. This is because Geminis are intellectual people and choose to think beyond their emotions. This characteristic allows them to forgive quickly.

Additionally, do not expect to go behind a Gemini's back and think that they will never find out about it. Geminis are very inquisitive characters. If they sense any secret, they will try to find it out. This is why you should always be honest and upfront with a Gemini. They will prefer honesty instead of a lie any day of the week. No matter how harsh the reality is, they will appreciate it.

Do Not Try to Control a Gemini

Geminis are free souls who are always in search of their big new adventure. Geminis do not like anyone navigating their life for them. They prefer exploring and finding their path in life. If you try to set restrictions on your partner or control them in any manner, then you might find your Gemini partner to be very unhappy. Allow them the freedom to explore the world on their own and be respectful of this decision of theirs but if you find Geminis lost and in trouble, then reach out to them and offer them your support. Geminis might like independence, but they also like companionship.

Do Not Take What a Gemini Says as Binding

You might notice that Geminis often act contradictorily. This is because their personalities are multi-dimensional, which often confuses them at times. So, if a Gemini tells you that they want to go on a walk tomorrow, then do not take it as a definite truth. They might wake up tomorrow morning and feel like going to the gym rather than on a walk. So, be aware of such possible scenarios occurring in your relationship. In these situations, rather than forcing their former decision on them, you should encourage them to pursue their new desires. If this situation extends to them canceling plans, then do not be upset. If it bothers you, then talk to them about how their behavior affects you. Accusing them of being unavailable and flaky will not be the right approach to this situation.

These were a few tips to keep in mind if you are in a relationship with a Gemini, but in the next chapter, we will discover a Gemini's compatibility with the rest of the zodiac signs. We will explore the relationship in a way that encompasses both the Gemini and the other zodiac signs. Be mindful that these are the traits that the sun suggests, but a conscientious effort from both parties can change the outcomes.

Love and Other Zodiac Signs: Compatibility, Obstacles, and Navigating Love

In astrology, predicting compatibility based on behavior which itself is assumed from the interaction of suns, moons, and planets, is quite big. People in huge numbers look at their horoscope and consider their compatibility with other zodiac signs when looking for a serious relationship but there is not any evidence to support the claims made in these charts.

They predict compatibility based on zodiac signs that emerged in the Western culture in the 1970s and are referred to as synastry. In this approach, the astrologer actively makes birth charts for each person through various methods. They then compare these birth charts to predict how well both the involved personalities will align.

The compatibility charts adopt a very popular approach when making predictions. They take into consideration the rising sign of each person. The rising sign refers to the zodiac sign that emerges from the eastern horizon at the time of a person's birth. Many also take into consideration the position of moons and planets, but to produce accurate predictions based on those positions, you have to know the exact time of birth, as the positions change with time. In this chapter, we look at compatibility based on the sun signs since looking at other factors will only complicate our understanding. We will look at what obstacles can arise in a relationship, how well two zodiac signs match in terms of love, and we will also look at how compatible they are in bed.

Every zodiac sign is unique and is defined by its traits. As discussed before, these traits play an important role in every person's love life as their ruling planet administers them. In this section, we will match Gemini with other zodiac signs and figure out how well their compatibility rates and find any obstacles that might arise. There are

---

twelve zodiac signs in total, and we will explore all, one after another. This might get long, so let us hurry up!

An Aries and a Gemini together is an interesting match. While Aries is an enthusiastic group of people, Gemini is psychologically gifted. A Gem will try to mimic the energy level and the passion of Aries, even though they might not feel that way intrinsically. While mimicking your behavior to fit in, they will ignore all the things you are condemned for (like being too angry) and focus on the good side of your personality (like your empathy). The Aries will dominate such relationships, but Gems will have no problem steering the wheel and will not hesitate to throw in their ideas and advice about what to do next. One best part about this relationship is that Gemini will not get offended easily. It is hard to offend them, and even when you do, they get over it quite easily. In modern relationships, most of the problems arise from one person disrespecting and offending the other. This will not be the case here (at least not for a Gem) as they are very thick-skinned and not a fan of holding grudges. Neither of these people are jealous, clingy, or emotionally over-demanding. An Aries will ignore the Gemini's sides that other people might usually point out and criticize them for, but the most significant challenge for these couples come from the lack of excitement to finish a venture. These people love starting a new project or a task in their life and lose the excitement midway. The allure of a new idea distracts them as they lose sight of what they have already started.

Taurus and Gemini might be a terrible match because it can end in an agonizing skirmish of demeanors in the relationship. A Taurus is usually tricky, but their stubbornness is accentuated when in a Gemini relationship; as discussed before, Gems are highly expressive and exceptionally lucid. This relationship might feel like a ball (Gemini) ricocheting off the wall (Taurus). Not only this, but Taurus does not reciprocate Geminis love of chaos. Gems loathe routine and are impatient people, while Taurus prefers a sense of organization. This might result in many arguments, but Gemini, being masters of negotiations and articulation, will have an edge in these too. This will further frustrate a Taurus who will lose an argument despite knowing that they were right. Moreover, it might be difficult for a Taurus to keep up with a Gem because they are active and social.

Although everyone appreciates hard work and dedication, no one likes chaos and rampant disregard for efficiency. This might also stretch to the bedroom where both of their sleep schedules might not match. Gemini's social personality might also not sit well with Taurus since they might not be as eager as a Gem on a night out. This might raise questions over commitment for Taurus, as on a night out alone, a Gem will not hesitate to talk to strangers at the bar or dance with someone on the dance floor. Taurus might fear that such actions might lead to something that can harm the relationship. If you want this relationship to work out, you need to be ready to make sacrifices and adjust. Compromise is important in this relationship, or you might find it too demanding and exhausting.

A Gemini and Gemini pairing is only suitable as long as it is limited to a friendship or casual flirting. The energetic personality and the chaos-loving character can often clash and accelerate the relationship to destruction. Being very active and hardworking, this couple might find themselves too busy to share alone time. Often romantic times might not be planned but rather occur naturally. Since both of these people will be disorganized and will be lacking passion, they might find themselves lost in the relationship. Figuring out where they stand in the relationship might be difficult, and both will be scared to commit to one another. It is possible that both of them might play mind games with one another and purposely and falsely lead each other on.

There has to be a person who can think emotionally and one that can be intellectual in a relationship. There is also a requirement for someone to entertain, so no one loses interest. When two of the same zodiac signs are brought together, their strengths and weaknesses are magnified, and this can influence the nature of the relationship. Since

Geminis are social creatures, together they can be amazing friends, but the lack of passion and emotion usually means they may not make a great romantic partner.

Cancer and Gemini relationships can either be excellent or end badly. Gems are entertaining human beings who are always searching for a little fun. On the other hand, Cancers are intuitive individuals and very empathetic. Cancers are usually reserved and try to keep their social circles small. Gems are social creatures, and this is why both their personality traits are clashing. On a date night, Cancers might prefer eating-in, while Gems might like to eat-out. Cancer can offer a sense of security to the partner and comfort them and give them the attention they need, while the Gem can be the source of adventure in the relationship, keeping it young and interesting. These different traits can provide a balance in that relationship that can, in actuality, work well, but this balance will not come naturally; rather, the couple will have to work on it. Similarly, clashes can arise because Gems prefer to be a free soul, while Cancers like their home and family. This means that a Gem might not be ready for commitment when Cancers are seeking it.

Fights might arise because Cancers can perceive Gems as emotionless, lacking empathy, and stubborn. At the same time, Gems can view Cancers as over-emotional and too needy. These differences will only resolve if both the people realize that each of them is different, and rather than getting angry, they try to learn from their differences. Acceptance will make the relationship last a lifetime.

Leos and Geminis are similar in many ways and also different in various fashions. Like Geminis, Leo is also very social and enjoys going out. They both want to be the topic of discussion and want the entire room to notice. This couple can have a nice time competing for the spotlight, but it can also lead to struggles as they both compete for the same thing. Being sociable, both of them are always looking for ways to entertain each other. They can have a good laugh in this relationship and feed off each other's positive vibe, but beware, because Leos can be dramatic and a little extravagant. Gems might not appreciate this behavior, as they value analytical behavior more than impulsive, let alone extravagant. Although Geminis might enjoy this trait eventually when traveling to new places with their Leo and benefiting from this trait's entertainment perspective. And most Leos take casual flirting quite well, but a few may not correctly interpret the intentions. So, Leos might be quicker in expecting commitment than Gemini. If this is to happen, it is better than you clear your intentions about flirting at the start of the relationship.

Another clear difference between both these zodiac signs is that Leos prefer organization and work hard to prevent chaos. The Gemini, as stated before, is disorganized and enjoys the thrill of a chaotic environment. Overall, this relationship is very compatible, both emotionally and physically.

Gemini and Virgo are both good communicators and can effectively convey their feelings and frame their arguments. They have very sharp minds and often think from the head, and do not allow their judgment to be clouded by emotions. Virgos are not clingy and are not excessively demanding in a relationship, but they might misinterpret a Gem's casual flirting with other humans. In such times they can become far more possessive than any other human being. The advantage of firmly framing your arguments and thinking rationally will allow you to resolve many conflicts in the relationship.

Virgos are very dedicated to their work and can stress about the deadlines and their duties. Arguments might occur because Gemini, being disorganized, might not take their concerns seriously. Moreover, Virgos might also come across as problematic, as they have the tendencies to critique and pick on minor details. Virgos are also big on smart spending. They like to make efficient use of their money and make their purchase decisions after quite a bit of thought. On the other hand, Gems are spontaneous and can make big purchases for the sake of the thrill. So, money can also contribute to conflicts in the relationship. Overall, they both make a great match since Virgos are down to earth and can tend to a Gemini's needs.

A Libra-Gemini relationship is a perfect relationship per the books. They both are very compatible with each other, and there are no downsides to pursuing this relationship. You need to be cautious about exhausting the spark in the relationship by over-using it. Geminis are flirty humans, but they might find "the one" in Libras. Both of these zodiac signs are intellectuals, and debates in this relationship will be interesting. Arguments might erupt through these debates, but people in this relationship will easily forgive each other. The love for travel and adventure is also common among both of these zodiac signs. Unless there is a storm outside, neither prefer to stay indoors. They like social gatherings and will eagerly join each other to go to events. Libra's enthusiasm and positivity will stand out to a Gemini, and these attributes will bring out the better in a Gem. When this relationship gets serious, Geminis should beware because Libras will be the first to think seriously of marriage. Gems are adventurous, but this time they will cave in. Being indecisive, marriage might take a long time arriving, but they both will come to this chapter sooner or later.

A Scorpio is often considered a dark personality, especially when its traits are looked at in isolation. So, this Scorpio-Gemini relationship might be a struggling battle since Gemini's are full of heart. As far as bedroom antics go, Scorpio makes a wonderful and fulfilling partner but there will be an evident emotional battle in the conflict. Scorpio signs are mysterious characters, and this will attract a Gemini to them, but this mysterious character also demands privacy. So, Gemini will have to respect their privacy; if not, then the Scorpio will erupt.

Scorpios are highly instinctive humans and also secretive, but they are good at understanding people and their intentions. Gemini might often find them talking to their partners in this relationship about their own troubles in order to seek Scorpio's advice since they are good with people and have an excellent understanding of their nature. Because of this intense trait of Scorpio, a Gem might find them too possessive. Similarly, Geminis might be perceived as immature because of their playful nature that is often on exhibition during the worst possible time. Also, Gems might not be bothered by how they are perceived, but Scorpios will be. Scorpio will also want to dominate the relationship and be in control. If there are not significant compromises made, this relationship will not last long, even considering it is a very unlikely match. Compromise and respecting each other is the only way to make it happen.

Geminis are naturally attracted to Sagittarius because of their personality, which happens to be quite fun. They are very inquisitive humans and prefer being in a social environment where their sharp intellect can be displayed. Both the people in this relationship like steering conversation toward enthralling topics, and communication between both the people will be great.

Geminis have a wide array of hobbies and interests, while Sagittarius likes to concentrate their interests and be very passionate about them. Each partner will likely introduce the other to newer interests and activities during this relationship but Sagittarius' personality trait of being open and blunt might be found annoying by many Gems. Sagittarius is very self-opinionated, while Gems try not to judge people and situations and be analytical rather than emotional. So, Sagittarius being bluntly honest might not be appreciated by many Gems and may cause conflicts in the relationship. Sagittarius prefers a civilized debate instead of the casual exchange of ideas. They might hold a Gemini responsible and at fault for not choosing a side and passionately defending an idea. This might cause a Gem to think of their partner as shallow, while Sagittarius might think of a Gem as irresponsible. Still, neither accusation is true about each other's personality traits. Whether these things annoy the people in this couple will unfold later in the relationship, but the couple will have a lot of fun. Both the zodiac signs are funny and outgoing. They love adventures and are always looking for something to do. They also have a similar sense of humor and can track sarcasm well. This is why the Gemini-Sagittarius relationship will always be energetic and have the spark despite the differences. According to the zodiac, both these people will be complete opposites of each other. This relationship will go well or will be a disaster. It will depend on how early they get bored with each other.

Capricorns are a very complicated personality. They are a combination of passion, hard work, humility, and determination. The Capricorn's sexy and entertaining side is reserved for their friends and loved ones, and they do not leave it on exhibition for anyone else. A Gemini might be only exposed to a serious personality, making them feel like a parent rather than a lover. Capricorn's ability to be focused on their goals and be very organized clashes with Gems' spontaneous and chaotic personality. Although a Capricorn can be sexy and romantic, they might express this emotion through a series of practical actions rather than plain cheesy and hopeless romantic behavior. This might cause a Gem to perceive a Capricorn as dull. This perception might also come to a Gem's mind because Capricorn handles money and lives their life with considerable care. Capricorns like to be careful with money and save for an unfortunate situation when it can help them. A Gem likes to spend it as it comes.

Additionally, Capricorns like a sense of predictability in their life and to know what is in store. They like to like to organize their every step and practice what they want to say in a conversation beforehand. So, they do not like spontaneous plans and socializing. Geminis, on the other hand, love going out and can go on a new adventure every day. Initially, Capricorns can expect to enjoy the light-hearted and entertaining personality of Gems. Still, it will soon fade out if none of the involved parties are ready to compromise or understand the other's personality. Sex will also be fun and cheery in the beginning, but that too will become too predictable and, thus, boring – especially for the Gemini.

Aquarius is a very confident and exciting bunch of people. They like to have deep conversations but also have a fun and entertaining side to them. They can be perceived as cold, but they are very intellectual and unpredictable in an entertaining fashion. This is the reason why an Aquarius-Gemini relationship will be perfect and should be pursued without any hesitation. Even if the relationship does not work out too well, the people will find lifelong friends in each other.

Geminis and Aquarius do not form opinions about another person because they do not care how people perceive them, and as a result, they do not judge people. The Aquarius and Gemini duo makes a great match because of this. Moreover, Aquarius finds the indecisive and chaos-loving nature of Geminis attractive rather than dull, unlike most of the other star signs. However, Aquarius can be a little reserved when expressing their commitments and romantic feelings to their partner. This trait might have been a threat to the relationship with a Scorpio, as they need continuous attention and validation from their partner. In the case of a Gemini-Aquarius relationship, this trait is harmless as both are not clingy and possessive. None of the people in this relationship will be emotional, and both like to have witty and intellectual debates.

Aquarius strives to be unique, and this trait will provide a thrill to the relationship since both like an adventure. This adventure will extend to the bedrooms too, where the Aquarius will be able to keep the Gemini on their toes romantically. This relationship will survive hardships and struggles as long as the personal boundaries of each person are respected. The only downside to this couple is that they both hate doing chores, but who cares when you are busy having adventures and making memories.

Pisces are very emotional and loving humans who think intuitively. A Gemini-Pisces relationship might not work out because of clashing personality traits. The very emotional character of Pisces is not compatible with the intellectual personality of Gemini. Gemini prefers to live their lives to their fullest by being adventurous and benefiting from the thrill that any situation can provide. They might find Pisces holding them back due to their demanding personality. In the relationship, Pisces will look for validation, and they will be needy for attention and love. Pisces can be passionate lovers and can be very unconditional, but Gems do not connect to deep and emotional love. Their idea of love is rooted in the emotional connection and the resulting friendship and joy. Because of this emotional love, Gemini will be repelled and back off from this relationship. This action will cause Pisces to feel insecure in the relationship and make them even needier for reciprocation and validation.

Gemini takes nothing seriously, while an Aquarius can have firm beliefs and can be too vulnerable and emotional about certain things and issues. This problem also extends to humor. Gemini's sense of humor can be possibly offensive for Pisces, as it can unintentionally hurt their sentiments. Geminis will, therefore, have to be very cautious around their partner. They might also find themselves turning around the mood of Pisces, who can be pessimistic and sad at times. Last, like Scorpio, Pisces, too, need their space to recharge for the day but unlike Scorpios, they do not do well in social settings, and a Gemini-Pisces couple might find themselves arguing about going out or not.

The above evaluations are made after considering the interaction between the sun signs. If you read the compatibility breakdown above and found that you are not best suited with someone you like, then do not be desperate. There are various other planets and astrological connections that can impact a relationship and can influence the compatibility between two zodiac signs. To better understand your compatibility, you can get an official astrological reading from an astrologist. If the answer is still the same as you find in this book, you can work on the differences mentioned and embrace them. Any relationship can be saved by respect and compromise.

A major part of a relationship is the intimate moments that you share together. When people search for a partner, they look for someone who can fulfill their emotional as well as physical needs. It can be challenging to keep a relationship afloat if one person values sex more in the relationship than the other person. Considering every partner's needs and catering to their needs is the crux of the relationship but in terms of sex, this can get difficult if one person in the relationship does not want to have sex while the other one does.

Many people often define a healthy relationship as the quality of sex that people are having in a relationship. Sex can be a deal maker or a deal-breaker for Gems when pursuing a relationship. Below, we will explore how the match of different zodiac signs fare in terms of compatibility when it comes to sex.

The sexual chemistry with a Gemini is not the best that Aries has experienced with their prior partners. Aries are people who need a certain sense of conflict to enhance their sexual urges. Aries-Gemini sexual chemistry will be intense, and the passion and creativity of the Aries will be welcomed and appreciated in the bedroom by a Gemini. Aries are also likely to dominate in the bedroom, and a Gemini will appreciate this dynamic. Gemini is excited by verbal lovers and will like it when Aries talk to them about their plans. Last, Gemini will also be more adaptive in the bedroom and become more daring to match an Aries' drive.

Gemini people are experts with their narratives in the bedroom, but this is not a Taurus' forte. Taurus is great at the physical act in bed but not at conversations, which Geminis like. Being adventurous, Geminis are also very experimental in the bedroom and will try everything at least once. They might prefer a quickie once in a while, and might try to break away from the routine to keep things interesting. This is something that a Taurus will be less likely to lean towards.

Being fun personalities, a Gemini-Gemini couple prefers light casual sex to something with a lot of emotions. They like stimulating their sexual desires through phone calls, texting, and acting. They might be perceived as superficial by other zodiac signs since they are repelled by emotional sex, but they will fully satisfy each other and will never get too clingy, allowing the other person to have their personal space.

Cancers like to have sex that has meaning, and which is deep and emotional. This clashes with the personality of a Gemini who prefers fun to emotions. Gemini's sexual desires might not be fully satisfied by Cancer because they might feel that their styles do not match. Similarly, Cancers might also feel dissatisfied. This dissatisfaction can be eliminated if they both appreciate each other better. Communicating with a Gemini when they need a cuddle can help Cancers. Similarly, if something is lacking for a Gemini, they can communicate it to their Cancer partner.

Leos and Geminis also have great chemistry in the bedroom. The sexual chemistry is great between them, as Leo loves when Gemini vividly pronounces their plans about what they wish to do in the bedroom. They both appreciate the light, sexual fun in the bedroom, which, as we have seen, is not reciprocated by many other zodiac signs. They both like being adventurous in the relationship and might experiment outdoors and indoors. This relation is a great start for a Gemini/Leo to overcome any manner of embarrassment or shame they face with their sex life.

For Virgos and Geminis, emotions in the bedroom do not matter, but this can be a problem as the sex might lack any form of intimacy in a Virgo-Gemini relationship, but this couple might also like this relationship because it is not needy and respects their personal space. Virgos can be a little too predictable for Gemini in terms of sex, and they might soon get bored with it. This couple also appreciates good phone sex or role-play. Geminis might take the dominator's role in the relationship while Virgo will be the submissive one.

The imaginative sense and the physical capabilities of a Libra and Gemini are so brilliant that they will certainly have a great time in the bedroom. Both of these people bring different dynamics to the bedroom. Libra brings romance into the relationship, while Gemini brings the aspect of adventure. This relationship will be characterized by fun role-playing before sex and various seductive games that will be the source of energy.

Although the emotions and passion of the Scorpio during sex complement the fun-loving approach towards sex by the Gemini, it will not last in the long run. Eventually, a Gemini might find this relationship to be too demanding, and the emotional aspect might be a massive turnoff for them. Scorpio and Gemini have opposing needs in bed, which might make sex unsatisfying for both parties after a time but understanding the needs of each other can deter you from experiencing such problems. It is not so bad to adjust, and it is not as self-sacrificing as it sounds. And Scorpios are very amenable to experimenting in bed, and their sense of spontaneity and unpredictability can keep things interesting.

Between a Gemini and Sagittarius, sex will be light and fun, and the couple will be very spontaneous and adventurous in their sexual encounter. They both equally enjoy experimentation in the bedroom and will try new things. This couple might take things out of the bedroom and involve themselves in risqué things. Both of these people are intellectuals and chatting will be part of the date, but sex will entail more than conversations in this relationship. Geminis love the sex drive of a Sagittarius, while the verbal aspect that Geminis bring to bed excites Sagittarius. This relationship can be molded into a long-term commitment if both the people make adjustments and think level-headedly. If things go smoothly, this couple also has chances of ending up married.

Capricorns and Gemini both love light-hearted sex, and this aspect will be appreciated in the relationship because there will be no restriction or expectations to behave. There will be extreme passion in the relationship, and Capricorns can teach a Gemini more about physical performance and push it to be more than just talk. Further, Capricorns have great stamina in the bedroom and can be very passionate when matched by the experimental nature of a Gemini, but there are chances that this passion will soon be overshadowed in the long term when feelings of dissatisfaction settle in.

Aquarius and Gemini will be a great match in bed since both of them are not very needy and clingy. They will take things at a fast pace and taking their clothes off will not take much time. They will start having sex very early on in the relationship. Additionally, these zodiac signs do not necessarily have to be in a relationship to have sex. They can be friends and occasionally also have sex without blurring the lines of friendship. They can also concoct very erotic tales for their bedroom due to their imaginative and creative traits. This means that both people can always maintain the excitement in the relationship. In short, they both are very compatible, both in and out of the bedroom.

Pisces like to have a deeper meaning and emotional bond when they are having sex, whereas a Gemini does not like when emotion is tied to sex. Rather, they like it fun and exploratory with no connection, but a lot of experimentation. This difference in what they consider as good sex often allows the passion to fade out soon. After a short term of having sexual intercourse, things start to get dissatisfying in the bedroom. When Gemini tries to be independent, it increases the insecurity experienced by a Pisces. This causes a Pisces to be needier, and a Gemini might not provide them the validation that they might be longing for. If the people involved in this relationship can think level-headedly and compromise to conform to the other's needs, this relationship can withstand many obstacles.

This will help you explore your love options if you think that sex makes up a considerable amount of your life and it's of significance to you. But like the previous section, this section is also based on the sun and does not take into account the birth time-specific aspects –planets and moon positions.

Chapter 5: The Social Gemini

Geminis have a unique persona that can lead them to have prosperous social lives. The following chapter discusses the entire social profile of Geminis. This entails a detailed analysis of different social situations and the Gemini relationship with other zodiac signs. Reading the following content can help Geminis navigate through tough social situations. This chapter is also essential if you have a Gemini companion in your life and you want to better understand them. You can pick up useful pointers that will eventually help you to grow your rapport with your Gemini friend.

The Social Map of a Gemini

By now, most of Geminis' common traits have been discussed, but this section will cover those traits relevant to social situations like parties. Social situations like the workplace will not be covered in this chapter as those are considered separate profiles discussed in future chapters.

Gemini has been described as the most social zodiac sign on the zodiac wheel due to its communication and curiosity traits. These traits lead them to build a sound relationship with the people around them. Interaction with their community is also part of their ruling house trait, so they do not have to look far for satisfying connections.

These connections mentally stimulate our Gemini subjects, so we have to look at something similar when we are looking at social situations, such as a party.

Depending on their birth charts, people inherit different traits from their signs/ruling planets. Most Geminis have this burning curiosity to know more about life. Keeping this in mind, it is safe to assume that Geminis are among the most extroverted people at a party. Geminis are often interested in the audience/participants at an event or party rather than the party itself. Their innate ability to communicate effortlessly is a gift that is used very wisely in such situations. Their ability to articulate well is one of their strongest suits and can get them through the worst misunderstandings in life.

Geminis also have the ability to adapt to different situations. They can rewire their brain more quickly than a few of the other signs if faced with a situation they were not prepared for, since they have basically faced their dual nature during their whole lives. Both of these abilities help in approaching random strangers and connecting with them at a human level. These traits make random interactions easy and natural for the Geminis.

An ideal night out for a Gemini involves bar hopping with a couple of their closest friends. They will always be open to thoughtful conversation at the bars in exchange for a few drinks. Engaging in conversation will satisfy their mind while the activity around them will make them feel as if they are in their most natural element. Whether a Gemini is single or not, they will always have a fun night out if it involved bar hopping activities.

Geminis have a couple of other traits as well that can help them navigate through a party. Geminis are independent souls; thus, they do not fear doing things on their own. This means that they want to do more than just dancing or drinking at a party. So, partying with them will contribute to a fuller experience rather than it just being a wasteful night that ends up giving you a hangover. Depending on their individuality and their house positioning (cusp positioning), Geminis may range from seeking a very wild party experience to a fuller experience, but one thing is for sure: no party is a dull party with a Gemini.

An ideal party for a Gemini will start off normally, like any other party but it is only a matter of time before the Gemini gets bored and leaves or does something to make it more interesting. A lot of interesting strangers should be part of the party so that the Gemini can exercise their traits and have thoughtful exchanges all night long. Another feature of an ideal party for the Gemini includes a lot of wild party games. "Wild," in this case means absolutely entertaining and fun, and in many cases, it can get immensely personal as well. The Gemini teens and adults like such games that bring out the personal details of a person's life since they are always looking for something interesting to chat about.

Another trait of social Gemini is to get involved in the gossip that goes around. Geminis will never admit this, but they love to gossip since that too is a part of communication, and it brings out many interesting details (from people's lives) to satisfy their mental cravings. As a Gemini, you can relate to this last detail wholeheartedly since we know you will not admit it to anyone else in reality.

A few Geminis (who have unique birth chart positioning) may not follow most of the traits explained above for a social setting. It depends on the cusps and houses that the astrologer draws out, but different activities can bring out the best of them at a party. Many can be carefree while others can decide to engage in activities only. It really depends on the individual's personality, but the basic traits of the Gemini may still be observed often.

Another factor decides how Geminis interact and behave with different people in a party (or a social setting). The zodiac sign of the person that you are interacting with also matters. Compatibility is a metric that astrologers often use to decide whether two signs will be compatible with different activities/stages in life, such as love, marriage, friendship, sex, and other similar things. We can examine the Gemini's relationship with each of their zodiac compatriots to see who will bring the best out of them. Our results will also show us why Geminis might react negatively to a person at a bar or at a party.

Gemini is very compatible with Aquarius as both have pretty similar traits and are looking for things that the other is willing to offer. They will never run out of topics to talk about and do share a few of the split personality traits, meaning they can shift from activity to activity throughout the party extracting the most fun from each one. Aquarius and Gemini make a good match in many aspects of life, and this social aspect can also yield a wholesome friendship between the two. They can link up pretty quickly but both of them rarely have similar feelings towards something.

Libra and Gemini both represent social people, so they will always have playful chemistry between them. They may even become best friends, but it may be a clash of two alphas at a party. Joining forces might make a lot of people jealous, and they may get looks from other people throughout the party. Libras may find this as validation, but Geminis have fairly different emotions, and so their emotions do not coincide.

Gemini and Aries are described to be more of a hot and cold match. During a party, the opposite aspects of their personalities can attract each other while other aspects may become a turnoff. This situation is when an air sign meets a fire sign, and it can get pretty adventurous and passionate really quickly.

Leo and Gemini are a few of the more egoistic signs, and their conversation can make both of them appreciate each other. Their differences are what attract each other, and so this too is a fire and air match.

Sagittarius and Gemini can have an instant connection based on how similar they are. They can be amazed at how similar they are once they talk at a party, but being too similar may not allow both of them to take this friendship further.

Gemini likes attention, and Taurus is one sign that is willing to give it. Interaction between them at a party is sure to bring out a fruitful relationship, but how long it will last can be questioned; however, it would be fulfilling for the moment.

Gemini and Pisces can form a unique connection that focuses on their creativity. At a party, they can go on and on about their creative sides. Both have different emotions and may not get each other in the long term.

Scorpios have an intense personality and are a straight challenge to Gemini's personality. Geminis can be intrigued or repelled by it but if they have an initial conversation that goes well during a party, then they have probably found someone who can keep them in check.

Cancer and Gemini have fairly positive compatibility because Geminis want to feel appreciated and want attention, and the Cancers can give it to them, but the Gemini's tendency to become uninterested fairly quickly might not allow this relationship to foster.

Capricorn and Gemini may not be the perfect partners in a relationship, but their connection can be pretty fun at a party. The Capricorn's posing will put off the Gemini, but their curiosity can carry them through an entire conversation. It might not be fun, but it will still be interesting.

The Gemini and Virgo combination is not the best connection that a Gemini can have at a party. Virgos have too many walls, and at first, the connection might be interesting, but the Gemini will eventually feel uninterested and run away from it.

Many of the best connections that a Gemini can have are with other fellow Geminis! This combination will be fun for the Geminis as well as everyone else at the party or at any other social situation. This is mainly due to how similar both of those people will be and how they will instantly make all of their life decisions. They will also relate to each other's lives, which might be the start of a budding friendship.

Gemini Friendships

Ever wondered why you cannot seem to start up a conversation with your Gemini classmate? There are a couple of straightforward ways for people to befriend Geminis, and this section will talk about a few of those ways. This section is also important for Geminis if they want to learn about how to make friends while navigating through their zodiac traits.

Geminis are not afraid to express their opinion, and so you are better off just initiating the conversation and let them take the driver's seat. Geminis are pretty confident, so complimenting them may work at first but building their self-esteem regularly will get you nowhere in the relationship. Try to contribute to the conversation by mentally stimulating them. You can do that by bringing in new debates and controversial opinions to prove them wrong. Geminis think that they are pretty smart (which may be wrong), and so debating with them is pretty fun. You can build nice chemistry by doing this, and eventually, Geminis are going to consider you as a fun indulgence. Doing so allows things to stay interesting, which will be an attractive proposition for the Geminis. Geminis will go wherever their curious mind takes them, so it'd be hard for them not to indulge in a fun and thought-provoking conversation where they are allowed to have the center stage.

Eventually, you can also help Geminis decide between two strong choices/opinions since they may find it really difficult to decide on their own. This will also add another layer to the dynamic of your relationship. You can give your own opinion about the two and then your final verdict for what they should choose. Such small things can also turn into a thought-provoking conversation that can keep the Gemini interested. Always remember to talk about different things as talking about the same thing is eventually going to bore them.

A common issue that people come across when trying to befriend a Gemini is their lack of interest in them, but Geminis might be preoccupied with other tasks as they are also described as a social butterfly. They do not just have a couple of close friends, but a lot of them, so you have to wait your turn and be patient with them. Once the thought of you pops in their mind, they are sure to respond positively. This is a common trait of the Gemini that people need to compromise on, as this is how they are hard-wired. You cannot change it; you can just be patient with it and reap this newly formed relationship's fruits.

Another pointer about befriending a Gemini is that if you want to spend time with them, you have to be ready for many movement activities. Geminis do not like to stay in one place for a very long time and so need a change of scenery every few hours. This is the effect of their trait of getting bored easily. Make sure to suggest any good places that you have in mind when they ask to move away from where you initially are. This way, you can control the situation, which might otherwise lead to someplace you do not find amusing. In this paragraph, the emphasis is on "suggest" as Geminis do not like being told what to do. Make it sound like it is a mutual idea, and hopefully, they will follow suit.

Geminis are pretty intelligent and easy to talk to, but if you are a Gemini, then you can relate to the next few tips that take you through the critical parts of maintaining your friendships. Geminis have a lot going on because of all the traits discussed in the guide, so it is difficult to focus on one relationship at a time. Their innate nature suggests having the excitement of knowing everything and talking to everyone. Knowing everything has its downfalls as you may cause relationships to fall apart by spilling secrets. As Geminis, this is something that is very hard to resist as they have a lot on their mind, and it is wired to communicate and articulate efficiently.

It is hard to keep your free-spirited nature in check, but if you focus on knowing less "secrets," then it will be easier for you to keep relationships. It is difficult to move a relationship forward without knowing intimate secrets about the other person, but it is possible. Many people do so and have been doing so for a while now. It is all about finding the right crowd who recognize your traits and then choose to tell you stuff even after knowing about them.

Another thing about you as a Gemini is that you always think about loving yourself first and may forget about your friends at times. This is because of two reasons. The first is that this is the innate nature of Geminis; they regard themselves as smarter individuals who deserve attention. This makes people feel like Geminis are narcissists, but that can be far from the truth. Perception is key, and in this case, it matters how you come across to others. The other reason why this is true is that you have so many friends that you may often neglect a few at times.

A straightforward tip for this case is to minimize your friend circle, but we all know that will not work for a Gemini. You should start to focus more on other people, especially your friends. This way, even when you are alone, you will be thinking about the small details they told you a few days ago. This way, you can always buildup relationships that you are focusing on rather than letting the good ones fly by. Many will think that they are being ghosted or ignored, and so they'll eventually stop making that effort of becoming your friend. Focusing on the smaller details and reciprocating them will show that you care about them and are making an effort to let them know that you love them.

More about all of these tips are covered in greater detail in the last chapter of this guide. The last chapter focuses on a Gemini's needs from the perspectives of a Gemini and an outsider so that better and prosperous relationships can be created.

Chapter 6: Gemini at Work

Professional career choices are a significant part of any person's life. Deciding what you intend to do for the rest of your life can be alarmingly difficult for anyone. In this book, we will be exploring the possible careers Gemini may adopt. We will be referring back to the strengths and weaknesses discussed earlier to understand the reasons behind a specific career discussed.

The ideal way towards sustenance and survival is to play your strengths. As discussed earlier, Geminis are natural conversationalists and highly adaptive, but they despise boredom and prefer exciting and challenging tasks to monotonous routine work. If you are a Gemini, you will do poorly at a job that you force yourself into. Geminis do what they genuinely want to do. They are known for doing their job with passion and dedication, but only if they enjoy doing it. At the same time, they struggle to make crucial decisions due to their indecisiveness and might be reckless at times. Before we dive deeper into careers suitable for Gemini, think about the possible careers that Geminis thrive at. Also, think of which jobs they might hate. What jobs do the Geminis you know of do? Are your Gemini friends playing to their strengths?

Best Career Options for Gemini

Following their creative and outspoken personality traits, Geminis will make excellent journalists. Excellent speaking skills will help them interact with many people they may come across in their professional work. Interviewing people of influence is likely to come easy to Geminis. Using their fascinating creativity, Geminis can come up with intriguing questions and perspectives. Any journalist is obligated to know the news inside and out. This is where Geminis can use their inquisitive nature and comprehensive researching skills. They can patiently observe a situation from all sorts of point-of-views and build questions and ideas as a product of their research.

Furthermore, journalism is not a boring or stagnant field. In our modern world, there is always something important happening in every country on the globe. So, Gemini journalists are rarely found bored with their work. They embrace the new daily occurrences gladly and work on them religiously. Being articulate with the pen as well as with the tongue is another strength Geminis can benefit from in this line of work. By gathering an expansive range of knowledge, Gemini journalists are more likely to get recognition and accreditation. Since they intuitively hate bias, they are also deemed credible. Anderson Cooper and Ian Fleming are two of the most famous Gemini journalists we know of. If you are a Gemini, it is recommended you try interviewing and researching for a time. Not only might you enjoy it, but you might also be good at it.

A profession similar to that of a journalist is a presenter. Television show hosts, news reporters, and live presenters are all jobs that Geminis are meant to thrive at. These occupations demand interpersonal skills and confidence, and Gemini seems to have those in abundance. Due to their proficient way of communication, many Gemini may even make better presenters than journalists.

Having a sweet spot for conversations, Geminis might end up learning multiple languages if they move to a foreign land. This potentially can make Geminis excellent translators. The ability to research extensively on a language may be tedious for the rest of us, while a Gemini may devotedly learn a new language. Multilingual people often make good ambassadors as well.

Another suitable profession for Geminis is a tour guide or travel vlogger. Gems love traveling around the world, from city to city. They love the freedom of expression as well as the freedom of mobility, and this job just might fulfill that. Being a good tour guide or travel-blogger requires resourcefulness, communication skills, and adaptability. Not surprisingly, Geminis check all those boxes. Being a tour guide is about being clear and kind with your tourists, something Geminis seem to be comfortable with. How can one forget the creativity of a Gemini when it comes to having fun? They will never leave their tourists bored and can be a treat to be with on an adventure. Moreover, Geminis tend to be comfortable in front of the camera and fully express themselves. Their love for exploring can take them to the farthest point from wherever they may stand.

Art is a field that will fully utilize the creativity of a Gemini. In our modern world, art can take various forms, including poetry, writing, videography, painting, and so on, but the commonality between all these is creativity, adaptability, and variety. Geminis tend to excel in these aspects and hence, usually do way better than other people as artists. Geminis with eloquent and melodic voices should lean towards becoming singers. Those who are praised for their witty humor should try their luck as comedians. Those who are quieter than their fellow Geminis should try drawing or painting to show their unfulfilled creativity. Acting is notably common amongst Geminis as it not only gives them a platform to showcase their communication skills but it adds excitement, challenges, and fame to a Geminis life. Did your high school recently host a theatrical play? See how many of those actors were Gemini. If we look at the Hollywood industry, a few of the most reputed names born as Gemini are Morgan Freeman, Kanye West, Paul McCartney, Prince, and Michael Moore.

Geminis also make amazing salespeople. They use their kind, energetic, and sociable personalities to convince potential customers. They see each person as a target and selling the products as their challenge. Being good social learners, they know when to step back and be respectful at the same time. Marketing also requires hectic surveys and research, something Gemini are reasonably good at. Be it getting their voice heard or getting their products sold, Geminis are gifted in both.

Another profession that Gemini can take up is that of a lawyer. A proficient and qualified lawyer can think differently, outside the box. The profession requires a substantial amount of research, learning, and exploring. Many lawyers continue to study even after cementing their industry position, as there is always something new to learn. Looking at this profession on the field, lawyers get bombarded with all kinds of different cases. A more empathetic Gemini lawyer can take on pro bono cases and help those in need. How can we forget the amount of public speaking skills a lawyer requires? A Gemini is sure to have the right attitude to become a lawyer.

The last career option we have for our fellow Gemini is the profession of a teacher. If you look closely, this profession seems to be perfect for a Gemini. Teaching requires the power of persuasive speech. Teachers should be able to communicate difficult topics to their students in the simplest form possible. Alongside that, they are obligated to get each student involved in the class discussion in one way or another.

As discussed earlier, Geminis are naturally outspoken, energetic personalities. They are capable of engaging the masses of students with the least compromise possible. Their active presence enables them to do anything to get the message across. They tend to develop enjoyable ideas and activities to enhance learning and convert a boring and dry class into an interesting one. Like university lectures or seminars and other higher levels, Gemini lecturers will relate to the young adults sitting in front of them. They are more likely to build healthy student-teacher relationships in a small amount of time with their students. The even better drive this profession may give to Geminis is the opportunity to interact with many young minds inside the classroom. Throughout their lives, Geminis hope to continue learning new things. This mindset is necessary for thriving as a teacher, which further strengthens Geminis as one of the best candidates for becoming teachers.

These were the professions that not only put fellow Geminis at an advantage but may also be fulfilling for them as human beings. It is perfectly fine if a Gemini opts for a career not discussed earlier. In the end, the case of choosing careers becomes subjective and depends on what a person truly feels and wants but there are a few professions that are not likely to be compatible with Gemini.

We know that Geminis are interested in an adventurous life. Gemini heavily dislikes any profession that ends up being monotonous in practice. Profitable and professional careers like accountants, bankers, clerks, factory workers, etc. tend to involve complex yet similar procedures every day. Professions that do not include a lot of communication or discussion are more than likely to put a Gemini to sleep instead of extracting rapid productivity from them. They always crave spice in their lives and run away from everyday office jobs. Ask around your Gemini friends who may be an accountant or a banker. Are they wholly content with what they do for a living? Chances are they might hesitantly say "no".

But it does not mean that Gemini will never make good bankers or office clerks. Being a Gemini provides you the ability to adapt quickly. If you are Gemini working at an office and seek excitement every day only to get disappointed, we recommend you be your workplace's life. Greet everyone with that bright smile of yours every day you walk in. Maybe treat your closest colleagues on a Saturday night after getting a proposal accepted. Leave a thank you note for everyone, from your boss to your janitor, to make his or her place as wholesome as you may like. You have the power and energy to uplift a crowd of people. Another tip is to make the best buddies at your workplace. This will, for sure, get you out of bed just to see their sparkling faces. Try decorating your workstation a bit with stickers and post-its if you are allowed.

Apart from the aforementioned career options, it is equally possible that another profession may intrigue you. Being loquacious beings, Gemini should find any career that lets them harness their raw interests. Look for careers that keep you entertained. Geminis adore a profession that allows them to teach and learn simultaneously. Had bad grades in academia? Do not worry. See if becoming a gym instructor or beauty trainer piques your interest. Geminis want a career that is both fun and productive at the same time. So, start by listing what is that you enjoy doing the most. When making career choices, ask yourself a few questions. Will I be consistently challenged while doing this? How will I be able to learn anything new through this job? Generally, try your best to get comfortable with your profession as quickly as you can. Only then can you truly excel in your career.

Compatibility with Your Colleagues

There is no denying that individual motivation, dedication, skill, and persistent hard work lie at the core of a professional's success. But to be able to contribute to a firm, society, organization, or even a small project, excellent teamwork and intelligent leadership are what really define the end product and its success. In this section, we will look at Gemini as potential leaders or bosses, as well as see how compatible they can be with their peers in the workplace.

By now, we know that Geminis are excellent with people. They tend to catch up with what their colleague's mood is, their likes, and dislikes. Their proficient interpersonal skill help keep their team gelled together for the entirety of the project but their weaknesses, like indecisiveness and inconsistency, may limit their progress in the long run. Keeping Gemini's characteristic traits in mind, let us discuss what a Gemini boss would be like.

A typical Gemini boss is likely to be an intelligent, innovative, yet impulsive workplace member. They arrive at work full of energy and tend to charm their workers with the sheer energy they bring. A Gemini will give his heart for the sake of their profession. Their passion for their work mainly fueled the effort and hard work they put in to reach that position in an organization. If a Gemini makes it to the top as a boss, no one doubts his or her commitment to their work line. So, their co-workers find them incredibly charming and inspiring. Looking at a Gemini boss and their loyalty should be enough to motivate the workers and employees around them.

When it comes to actual practical work, Gemini bosses prefer verbal collaborations and constant feedback. They are likely to have early morning meetings and multiple discussions throughout the day. Every worker and employee will have a say in a meeting led by Gemini bosses. During these meetings, it may seem like everyone is the boss because of the amount of attention the Gemini boss gives them. Are you working under a Gemini boss? You are likely to get tired of the number of meetings they may call everyone in for, but these collaborations and conferences keep a Gemini going at work. The exchange of ideas, discussion, critique, and diverse set of insights fill their tank of information, which they need to make decisions. The more information a Gemini boss has, the better chances are of their decisions of being effective and efficient. Apart from sharing and learning insights, Gemini bosses regularly celebrate small successes to keep everyone motivated. The discussions may even conveniently shift from productive work-related meetings to chatty personal conversations. This probably stems from the eternal hate that Geminis have for monotonous working environments.

Geminis believe in teamwork more than individual brilliance but that does not mean that they restrict their workers to the ideas of the masses. Geminis hate being micro-managers and dictating to their employees. They despise the conventional dogmatic style of management at work. Under a Gemini boss, workers tend to have full control over how to go about their tasks, as long as they deliver effectively and in a timely fashion. If anyone wants creative freedom at work, they will thrive working under a Gemini boss. This may be because Geminis themselves crave creative freedom at work. They do not like being strictly instructed on doing their job and continue reflecting the same when they become bosses. Many Gemini bosses may even have a special group of people to deal with less important responsibilities. They may be delegated full or majority of the control over many tasks while retaining their say in final decisions.

One of the biggest strengths of being a Gemini boss is being able to carry the team together for the project's length. Gemini bosses thrive in communication and are also open to ideas and proposals. They want to be continuously updated on any news that may have taken place. Most Gemini bosses have an open-door policy. Just came up with an idea you think will benefit the project? Walk straight into your Gemini boss's office. He will be ready and open to hearing your propositions.

Geminis are able to keep their workers motivated easily. They tend to appreciate small things like regularity and a sense of initiative a worker may show. They celebrate their personal joys to develop their sense of belonging at work. They also encourage their workers to interact with each other as much as they can. They might assign a task to two separate departments to increase productivity and let their workers get to know each other. This is beneficial for a project, especially one that consists of a lot of collaborative tasks. Thanks to the Gemini boss, the overall chemistry between the workers improves, and the project flourishes.

A Gemini boss is very comfortable when it comes to solving the company's urgent problems and overcoming unforeseen hurdles. They can improvise and adjust when it comes to sudden changes in situations. With their diverse knowledge and experience, they are able to figure out a way through excruciating circumstances. A Gemini boss champions anyone when it comes to reacting to emergencies. They are quick to give valuable suggestions and keenly analyze what others have to say. This makes Gemini bosses excellent managers during a crisis. They do not panic under pressure and keep themselves composed while working.

While Gemini bosses may not be strict managers, they are amazing observers. Being committed to their job, they are peerless when it comes to analyzing and keeping track of the activities of those working under them. They are quick to point out and discuss the mistake made by their team workers and calmly communicate and rectify it with the one at fault. While it may be a little embarrassing to be observed and critiqued at work, employees working under Gemini bosses progress and improve comfortably than the rest. If they start looking up to the Gemini boss as a mentor, they will notice significant growth in their professionalism and productivity at work. In short, those working under a Gemini boss are on a shortcut to self-improvement.

One of the best things about the Gemini bosses is that they create a gratifying workplace experience. Geminis themselves prefer fun in parts of their lives, which is reflected when they become bosses. A Gemini boss thrives in work that he enjoys and believes the same to be true for his or her workers. They may occasionally have games night or contests with rewards for the winner. Apart from motivating every member under them, they will individually socialize with them for hours. Furthermore, most Gemini bosses themselves lead very social and extroverted lives. They tend to have a lot of fun, so anyone will want to work for them because it is enjoyable.

But just like any human being, Gemini bosses are likely to struggle in certain ways. They have a few weaknesses that they need to work on to get the best out of themselves and their profession.

Gemini bosses tend to change directions and shift priorities throughout the process. They are flexible in managing these changes. They tend to react quickly to changes, and that may lead to a variety of different decisions in a short time. They may appear to be undisciplined and inconsistent with their workers. While this practice may have the benefit of keeping the workers on their toes, it tends to be annoying and exhausting. Hence, working under a Gemini is often difficult. The workers may not know what to expect every week. If you are someone who prefers the conventional dogmatic methods of working, you are likely to struggle to sync with your Gemini boss. Do you or know someone who works under a Gemini? Notice how frenzied the routine working under them can be. This inconsistency is what may make a Gemini boss less effective as a leader. No matter how much they try to keep everyone on the same page, they might leave people behind in the hustle and bustle. If you are a Gemini boss, you should be extra careful not to overload work on those under you. Try to work on your consistency if you find it hampering the productivity of your workers.

Gemini bosses are always prone to be distracted. They do well at work only when they are devoted and concerned about it. If they fail to keep themselves motivated in a project, they will probably seek that thrill elsewhere. This may lead to sloppy and miscalculated decisions, which can prove to be painful to the workers and the project itself. Procrastination, random trips, and delays in meetings are likely to get a Gemini boss fired by those higher in the hierarchy. To deal with this shortcoming, Gemini bosses should have a personal assistant or an employee whose job is to keep them on track and get rid of any distractions. A good friendship with an equally motivated individual from the workplace can also prevent a Gemini from falling astray.

Other than this, Geminis themselves should continue with their jolly ways at work to keep themselves interested and devoted.

We know that Gemini bosses are not the perfect leaders. So, they need an exceptional team and the right environment to lead a project. If you work at an office or firm under a Gemini boss, you can always be sure to have an exciting and thrilling day, but it can also get difficult to deal with them at times. In those situations, the best choice is to go and calmly talk with your Gemini boss. They are good listeners and empathetic people and will tend to any concerns you may have. If we have learned one thing, it is that Gemini bosses and their workers all should be equally driven to work to be compatible with one another.

It is more than likely that Geminis may not end up becoming the boss of any team in their professional careers. In those cases, they may end up and employees and collaborators on a project. To know your compatibility with everyone may be exhausting and almost impossible but we have made it easier for you, as in this section, we look at how compatible Geminis are with other astrological signs at the workplace.

The first compatibility we will check is between Gemini and Aries. Aries are people born between March 20th and April 19th. Usually, Gemini and Aries get along very well. Both tend to have extremely energetic and adventurous personalities. If motivated by the same cause, they are most likely to have common ground and work together but there may be instances where Gemini and Aries might find problems working together in a partnership. When working with an Aries colleague, Gemini should be careful of maintaining their space at professional work. Since both have curious personalities, they are likely to bump into each other's work when working on the same project. When sharing your ideas with an Aries, a Gemini should be careful of presenting only an excerpt of concepts. Having long discussions on a variety of ideas can lead to a lot of wasted time, as Aries might not take things seriously.

Geminis have creative and inquisitive minds, which can help them to come up with brilliant ideas. On the other hand, Aries are energetic people who might do an excellent job in carrying out the plans a Gemini envisions. By complementing each other and rectifying each other's mistakes, Aries and Gemini can form a healthy professional partnership. If you are a Gemini with an exciting business idea, it is in your best interest to partner up with an Aries to get the job done. Profession-wise, Aries and Gemini will work together very well as marketers or salespersons.

People born between April 19th and May 29th belong to the astrological sign called Taurus. When it comes to working with a Taurus, Gemini might feel like dropping out of the partnership instantly. Taurus people are usually industrious, cautious, and pragmatic. They are dogmatic about the way of doing things. On the other hand, Geminis are adventurous and creative people who seek excitement at work. Both seem to have opposite personalities. While a Gemini will prefer multitasking, a Taurus will strictly adhere to their rules of performing one task at a time. Similarly, a Taurus might not welcome the open-mindedness a Gemini may offer. In practicality, it may be very difficult to build and fuel a healthy partnership between Gemini and Taurus at work but by bringing opposing ideas to the table, they can benefit from one another. For example, a Gemini might work on new creative ideas for marketing their product, while a Taurus will manage the hectic day-to-day activities like accounts, orders, finances, etc.

As we discussed earlier, Gemini is a sign of duality. So, having two Geminis on board is equal to having four people on your team. A partnership between two Geminis might lead to a lot of confusion and arguments. Both the Geminis will function as an idea creation machine. You can never run out of ideas with two Geminis in your office, but it is equally likely that both may debate on which, out of the many ideas they come up with, will be the perfect one. To a third person, two Geminis working together might look like two little siblings fighting over the last piece of cake, but these fellow Geminis will thrive under these fanatical conditions. To be able to collaborate effectively, a team of two Geminis will need a supervisor. Loss of excitement at work will mean a fall in the productivity of both the Geminis. If you are a Gemini at a workplace with another Gemini, you can always switch duties rather than starving from boredom.

People born between June 21st and July 22nd are born under the astrological sign of Cancer. If you thought Taurus was the opposite of Gemini, you were slightly off the mark. Cancers are people who prefer security and insurance instead of anything else. They tend to be conservative and introverted in nature when meeting new people. Meeting a Gemini can be an overwhelming experience for a Cancer, especially if the Gemini straight away handles the long-term goals while Cancer focuses on the ideas and other day-to-day activities by themselves. One shortcoming of this partnership will be that both are prone to overlooking small mistakes that can compromise the project's success.

Capricorns are people born between December 21st and January 21st. Capricorns are consistent, regular, sincere, and professional people, especially in their line of work. They are very strict about deadlines and try their best to deliver on time. Furthermore, Capricorns demand respect from their peers. They are quick to react to insults and jokes about them. At the same time, they know how to appreciate others when they see sincere dedication and productivity.

A partnership between a Gemini and Capricorn is unlikely to work out due to the difference in personalities. Being respectful is necessary to work with a Capricorn. Since Gemini tend to be talkative, they are most likely to annoy a Capricorn. A casual joke by Gemini can hamper the partnership but if both the Gemini and the Capricorn understand each other and be considerate, they can pull off tremendous accomplishments together.

People born between January 21st and February 20th fall under the astrological sign of Aquarius. Aquarius is known for its visionaries and thinkers. They believe that sheer will is the most fundamental driving force behind any accomplishment. They are sincerely dedicated to their vision and do not compromise on any obstacle that may interfere. These qualities make the partnership between a Gemini and an Aquarius unstoppable. Both Gemini and Aquarius aspire to achieve a range of things in their lives. While Gemini may lack the motivation to work, Aquarians are the perfect people to refill their tank. This partnership can bring forward a lot of influential ideas. If both Gemini and Aquarius are on the same page, they can achieve incredible success. One shortcoming of this partnership is the lack of practicality and an excess of idealism. Both Aquarius and Gemini tend to float around in a pool of incredible thoughts, but they lack when it comes to meticulous planning and implementation. This may lead to a waste of a lot of hard work. Nevertheless, both Gemini and Aquarius are likely to get along well and accomplish success with mutual optimism. The best collaboration between the two will have the Aquarius sort the long-term projects, while the Gemini deals with the day-to-day activities.

Pisces are people born between February 20th and March 20th. Similar to a Taurus, Pisces are introverted people who like to work silently on creative projects. While Gemini may announce their lives to them, Pisces will still stay reserved and mysterious to their colleagues. This may not be good for the partnership with a Gemini, who will then get bored and demotivated to work with their colleague. Pisces also demand freedom while working. This will not be good news for their Gemini partner because they will be left without someone to discuss or plan with. Overall, the two signs are not compatible to work together at a workplace but both Gemini and Pisces are known to be creative people. If somehow their ideas and imaginations coincide, a partnership between them can work out. With compromise and mutual understanding, they both can be teamed up to carry out a task.

While astrological signs may or may not be compatible together at times, one can always work out a relationship with the other through mutual compromise and understanding. If you are a Gemini, try reaching out to your fellow Taurus and Capricorn colleagues. Sit and talk with them. No relationship is impossible.

In this chapter, we extensively discussed possible careers perfect for fellow Geminis. We also saw how compatible they might be with peers at their workplace, with regard to the astrological sign to which they may belong. This chapter's purpose was to inform you more about yourself and others as members of the workplace. We highly recommend our readers to use the teachings to understand one another and figure out ways to work together.

Chapter 7: What Does the Gemini Need?

Being such a complicated personality, where they often have more than two personas, Geminis can often confuse themselves. As mentioned in the earlier chapters, these obstacles can hinder their experiences as children, at work, and as lovers. Although all the personality traits, be it a Gemini or any other zodiac sign, should be taken as a strength and celebrated, they can often make things difficult when not suppressed or altered according to their situation. For example, if someone is in a long-term relationship, they cannot shy away from commitment because there has to come a time when their relationship's fate will rely on their attitudes towards commitment. Sometimes, people do not realize the impact their characteristics can have on a person or a situation.

This book has covered the attitudes and actions of a Gemini in a workplace, at a social gathering, as a child, and as a lover. We have also discussed the compatibility of the Gemini with other zodiac signs, allowing them to smoothly manage their love life and choose their partners after educating themselves about what they will offer and how they will impact them, but we have yet to discuss how a Gemini can work around their personality's difficult parts. This chapter is designed to do so. Here we will explore various tips that can allow a Gemini to be a better human being by emphasizing traits that can give rise to problems or tension. We will also be looking at this aspect from the perspective of a friend or a loved one. We will explore how they can help a Gemini get around those personality traits and fashion a better situation. This will also inform them of any expectations they should keep in mind during an interaction with a Gemini.

For a Gemini

- Use Your Intelligence

Geminis are very gifted individuals with great intellect. They are equipped to think better than most people and have a higher IQ than most of the people. Being an air sign, they are very quick at thinking and are great learners, but they have no sense of organization despite this gift. Their smart and charming personality can allow them to achieve huge success in their future life, but this is compromised when they procrastinate and do not commit to the long-term. This is where they need to use their intelligence and make their decision strategically. Planning and structuring their future can safeguard them from the unexpected turns and bumps that life has to offer. Their spontaneity and adventurous nature are a defining trait of their personality, but they should only be explored in situations where they do not face a significant trade-off. Securing a well-paying job can offer them opportunities to explore more countries and experience more things. They need to clearly draw a line where this adventurous behavior is acceptable and does not compromise the quality and opportunities of their life.

- Don't Fear Emotions

Geminis have a dual faceted personality, which can make them contradict themselves. They also have an outgoing personality, which allows them to meet people and experience things that someone of another zodiac sign might miss out on. Their easy-going personality will enable them to be a good co-worker and an approachable person, but Gemini does not like emotional connections. This trait might sometimes be appreciated, but it can also make them lose out on friendships and relationships that need a certain sense of emotional reciprocation. Although valuing intellect over emotions is great for arguments, a small ounce of emotions needs to be introduced in relationships and friendship. They need to be emotionally present to appease other people and make them feel like they care. This will allow them to hold on to ties for a long time.

- Don't Be Indecisive

Being a mutable sign, Gemini often questions a decision. One personality suggests that they should do it, while their other personality pushes them away from the decision. This indecisiveness is also birthed from the fear of the repercussions that they might face if they make the wrong choice. Geminis need to let go of this fear and allow their adventurous trait to overtake their fear of eradicating indecisiveness. If a Gemini has a strong instinct favoring one decision over another, they should go for it.

- Keep Your Moodiness in Check

Moody behavior is also a product of the twin personality trait of a Gemini. They might find themselves switching from one decision to another and changing their emotions regularly but do not confuse this with them having any "bi-polar" tendencies; it's just that they can quickly change how they think. This behavior can extend to changing a date plan with a girlfriend at the very last moment, but this behavior is not just limited to changing plans. A Gemini needs to keep other people's emotions in mind when making sudden changes and when experiencing mood swings.

- Keep Your Sarcasm to a Minimum

Geminis are quick and witty individuals with a great sense of humor. This is the reason why they get along with so many people and can be the center of attention wherever they go. Their humor also employs a lot of sarcasm that might be misinterpreted by many people. A Gemini should stay considerate in order not to offend anyone. They can play down their sarcasm in a setting where they realize their sarcasm might not be fully understood. Instead, they can keep the conversation fun and cheery and allow their humor to be comparatively gentle.

- Don't Keep Secrets

Every person has secrets that they are trying hard to hide from people. These things are something that people are not proud, of but the decision to tell these secrets or keep them solely relies on the individual. But one has to realize that by letting go of secrets, they are in a way freeing themselves of the fear, restriction, or anxiety that it might be causing. Geminis being very happy and disconnected from emotions, tend to have a lot of secrets. Keeping these secrets can be very emotionally taxing and might consume a lot of their energy. Geminis might be missing out on fully living their lives solely because they are too scared to let go of these secrets. Emotionally opening up to people and sharing your personal secrets with them will allow a Gemini to live life more adventurously and freely than they now are.

- Prepare Before a Meeting

Geminis need an intellectually stimulating conversation to vibe with. So, prepare a witty or funny dialogue that you can start to allow a Gemini to take an interest in you. This will also make you be on the same wavelength as a Gemini. If you do not have anything prepared, do not worry. Just ask the Gemini questions from the conversation they are having. Questions appeal to the curiosity of a Gemini, and they will make you part of their conversation. You can use this tip to get to know a Gemini better and become friends with them.

- Be Acceptable

Gemini is a mutable sign; their double personalities can often make them appear to be inconsistent human beings. As stated before, they can have mood swings and suddenly change plans. Their tendency to say one thing and act on another might frustrate many people, especially those close to them but friends have to accept a

Gemini for who they are and look at the positive traits. This dual personality trait also means that Geminis are very adaptable human beings who reform their attitudes to fit in with different people. For example, in a posh setting, they might carefully present themselves while being very cheery and loud in a group of friends.

- Ignore Immature Behavior

Geminis love to be the center of attention and relish making people laugh. Although they are very intellectual people, they can be silly and loud in a social setting, like at parties. Many people might perceive their entertaining gestures as superficial and overly flirtatious. They will actively try to impress people and get a laugh out of them, but those who do not share the same humor might be bothered by it. If a Gemini is failing to suppress their sarcastic humor in such a setting, people who do not like such behavior should try to ignore it. If their actions bother you, then divert your attention to somewhere or something else. Gemini does not intentionally mean to bother or offend people, so try to understand them and not hold this against them.

- They Have Other Friends

Geminis are naturally very extroverted people, and this has been proven and verified through evidence and research. They love making conversations and interacting with humans. They are always on the lookout for change and can get bored easily with relationships and people. This is why you should keep a considerable number of friends and acquaintances and not heavily rely on a Gemini company. You should not feel offended if a Gemini is not answering your calls or replying to your texts because they might be occupied with another adventure. They will come back around when they feel like it is the right time for them.

- Don't Tell Them Your Secrets

Sharing a secret with a Gemini is one of the bad decisions that you might make. Thinking that a Gemini will hold on to your secret until the end of time is a wrong perception that you have. Being very social and interacting with many people, the secret might intentionally or unintentionally slip out of a Gemini. If it is intentional, then it will not have slipped out of malice, but rather as gossip that is too interesting not to hold a conversation about.

These were a few of the things that a friend with a Gemini should be mindful of. The purpose of these tips is to smooth the relationship that you have with a Gemini so that any arguments or misunderstandings can be identified and deterred easily. These tips will allow you to strengthen the bond and understand a Gemini at a much deeper level than anyone else.

Conclusion

We started with the horoscope phenomena and ended on a positive note about how relationships could prosper if people focused on their zodiac signs. As you can now confirm, there is a lot more to the zodiac than people initially suppose. All the inner workings have been communicated in the introduction. Readers must familiarize themselves with the introduction as it can be extrapolated to all zodiac signs on the zodiac wheel. The best chunk of information has been summarized to only the important details in the introduction so as not to compromise readability. Information about ruling planets, houses, cusps, natal charts, and gemstones has all been covered to show the astrologers' inner workings. An immense amount of mathematic application is required on the part of astrologers to make just one prediction. After reading this guide, Geminis can confirm that there is a bit of truth to all of those predictions.

The focus of this guide was on the different profiles that have been discussed in the book. From a human's birth to living out their entire life, all the profiles have been discussed in great detail. An entire chapter has been dedicated to each profile just so all the different perspectives about that profile can be cleared up.

This guide has tried to cover both perspectives that exist around this sign. The first one is about the Geminis themselves, while the second one is about the perspectives of the other signs. This allows the guide to be more complete than any other resource available on a similar topic. This is the ultimate guide to the zodiac sign known as Gemini!

Here's another book by Mari Silva that you might like

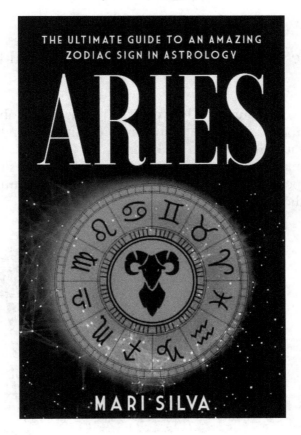

Your Free Gift (only available for a limited time)

Thanks for getting this book! If you want to learn more about various spirituality topics, then join Mari Silva's community and get a free guided meditation MP3 for awakening your third eye. This guided meditation mp3 is designed to open and strengthen ones third eye so you can experience a higher state of consciousness. Simply visit the link below the image to get started.

https://spiritualityspot.com/meditation

References

Astro Dentist. (2020). Frequently asked questions. Retrieved from https://www.astro.com:

https://www.astro.com/faq/fq_fh_owhouse_e.htm

Astrology Fix. (n.d.). Expert Gemini Guide. Retrieved from https://www.astrologyfix.com:

https://www.astrologyfix.com/zodiac-signs/gemini/

Baby Centre. (2020). Gemini Child. Retrieved from https://www.babycentre.co.uk:

https://www.babycentre.co.uk/h1029254/gemini-child

buildingbeautifulsouls.com. (2020). Gemini Childe: Traits, Personality, and Characteristics. Retrieved from https://www.buildingbeautifulsouls.com/zodiac-signs/zodiac-signs-kids/gemini-child-traits-characteristics-personality/

C.Ht., P. L. (2020). Traits of a Gemini Boss. Retrieved from https://horoscopes.lovetoknow.com/astrology-signs-personality/traits-gemini-boss

Chung, A. (2020). Compatibility Chart for Zodiac Signs. Retrieved from https://www.verywellmind.com/zodiac-compatibility-chart-4177219#history-of-astrology

Compatible Astrology, Staff. (2018). Gemini in Love. Retrieved from https://www.compatible-astrology.com/gemini-in-love.html

Green, T. (2017). 10 POWERFUL TIPS TO LEAD GEMINI TO SUCCESS. Retrieved from

https://astrologyanswers.com/article/gemini-zodiac-sign-success-tips/

Guerra, S. (2020). Top 5 Gemini Negative Traits You Need To Know. Retrieved from

https://www.preparingforpeace.org/gemini/negative-traits/#What_are_Gemini_Bad_Traits

Horoscope.com. (2018). Top 10 Careers For Gemini. Retrieved from

https://www.horoscope.com/article/top-10-careers-for-gemini/

Meade, J. (2019). Ranking The Zodiac Signs By Who Is Most Compatible With A Gemini. Retrieved from https://thoughtcatalog.com/jennifer-meade/2018/06/ranking-the-zodiac-signs-by-who-is-most-compatible-with-a-gemini/

Melorra. (2020). Zodiacal Gemstones - Gems as per Zodiac Signs. Retrieved from

https://www.melorra.com/jewellery-guide-education/gemstone/which-is-good-for/gemstones-by-zodiac-signs/

Middleton, V. (2019). A Beginner's Guide to Astrology. Retrieved from

https://www.thethirlby.com/camp-thirlby-diary/2019/5/22/a-beginners-guide-to-astrology

PeacefulMind.com. (n.d.). Air. Retrieved from https://www.peacefulmind.com/project/air/

preparingforpeace.org. (2020). Top 5 Gemini Positive Traits You Need To Know – Full Astrology Guide. Retrieved from https://www.preparingforpeace.org/gemini/positive-traits/

Prince, E. H. (2018). Six essential tips for dating a Gemini. Retrieved from

https://www.dazeddigital.com/life-culture/article/40376/1/dating-a-gemini-astrology

SCHAEFFER, A. (2020). How to Get Along With a Gemini. Retrieved from

https://classroom.synonym.com/get-along-gemini-4523008.html

Seigel, D. (2020). The 7 Fundamental Gemini Traits, Explained. Retrieved from

https://blog.prepscholar.com/gemini-traits

Tarot.com. (2020). Gemini Work Compatibility: The Thrill Seeker. Retrieved from

https://www.tarot.com/astrology/compatibility/work/gemini

The Finder, Staff. (2019). The Ultimate Guide On How To FIND LOVE According To Your Horoscope. Retrieved from https://thefinder.life/healthy-living/the-ultimate-guide-how-find-love-according-your-horoscope/